SAILING ACROSS THE SEAS

Fujian and the West

www.royalcollins.com

ILLUSTRATED FUJIAN AND THE MARITIME SILK ROAD

SAILING ACROSS THE SEAS

Fujian and the West

Wu Weiwei

Edited by Xie Bizhen

Books Beyond Boundaries

ROYAL COLLINS

Sailing across the Seas:
Fujian and the West

Wu Weiwei
Edited by Xie Bizhen

Translated by Daniel McRyan

First published in 2023 by Royal Collins Publishing Group Inc.
Groupe Publication Royal Collins Inc.
BKM Royalcollins Publishers Private Limited

Headquarters: 550-555 boul. René-Lévesque O Montréal (Québec) H2Z1B1 Canada
India office: 805 Hemkunt House, 8th Floor, Rajendra Place, New Delhi 110 008

ISBN: 978-1-4878-1125-9

To find out more about our publications, please visit www.royalcollins.com.

Foreword

As early as the 1st century BC, China had established an entire sea route from Xuwen and Hepu of Guangdong Province in southeastern China to the east coast of India; however, the early Chinese navigation was rarely related to the country's economic development. Emperors launched navigations to seek either the elixir of immortality or overseas treasures to maintain the luxurious and decadent lifestyle in the palace. The real overseas trade of China commenced when the Bureau of Foreign Shipping was set up in the Tang Dynasty. It was not until then that overseas trade was included in the national fiscal revenue.

Thanks to its superior geographical condition, Fujian is destined to play a significant role in the history of the overseas transportation and trade of China.

When the Maritime Silk Road is mentioned today, the descriptions tend to paint an easy and poetic picture. However, the formation of the Maritime Silk Road in history has gone through years of thick and thin. The merciless sea had devoured countless lives before the winding Maritime Silk Road came into being. As we look back on its development, we must not forget those great pioneers, namely, the monks who crossed the sea, the common people who went to sea to scrape out a living, the soldiers who went to war abroad, the envoys who were sent overseas, the courtiers who took refuge in foreign countries, the survivors of the shipwrecks, and the crew of Zheng He, who led seven voyages to the West.

It was commonly believed that Fujian ships were the best of all in the Song Dynasty. It was because Fujian had the most advanced navigation and shipbuilding technology of the time that the Quanzhou port had tremendous prosperity. The compass was widely used in navigation and nautical astronomy was developed. The stars were the guide and the wind the fuel. Navigation guidebooks were written and maps were drawn and passed down for generations. The advanced Western technology was also widely adopted in the navigation of Fujian sailors, such as the hourglass and the telescope. Their concept of navigation was evolving rapidly. The saying that "the sea is where Fujian people farm" pinpoints that they sailed for economic benefits. And the leverage of the economy drove them to open the age of Chinese exploration, where voyages were made all over the world and goods shipped overseas.

As per the existing historical data, the footprints of Fujian maritime merchants have been found in Japan and the Korean Peninsula, Southeast Asia, South Asian countries and the African continent. Business people from foreign countries also took Fujian ports as their footholds of trade. Historical documents have recorded that foreign merchant vessels trading with Fujian came from Asia, Africa, Europe, and America. The ancient Maritime Silk Road of China was a joint construction by the people of all countries in the world.

We admire the perfection of the ancient Maritime Silk Road, scrutinize the history of the navigation of Fujian sailors, and respect the outstanding contribution of Fujian ancestors to China's navigation. Their extraordinary sailing activities have left us abundant treasure, such as the sunken ships in the deep ocean, the traded goods that were found everywhere, the harbors silent for many years, the vaguely recognizable buoys, the long navigation picture scrolls, the yellowing nautical guide manuals, and the Mazu temples. The compilation of the illustrated series *Fujian and the Maritime Silk Road* aims to gather these scattered historical fragments piece by piece, so that a full picture of the historical record of Fujian on the ancient Maritime Silk Road can be seen.

The history of the development of the ancient Maritime Silk Road has pinpointed that the Maritime Silk Road came into being thanks to both Chinese and the people of various countries and regions along the way. Now, China's proposal to jointly build the Maritime Silk Road of the 21st Century conforms to the trend of world multi-polarization, economic globalization, and social informatization. Conducive to promoting the orderly and free flow of economic elements, it conforms to the fundamental interests of both China and the international community, highlights the common ideal and pursuit of the human society, and will inject positive energy to the world development.

Reviewing the history of Fujian and the Maritime Silk Road enables us to understand that in the process of building the Maritime Silk Road of the 21st Century, China should make an effort to enhance its comprehensive national strength, develop a value system attractive to all countries, create real soft power, and build its international image and prestige, so as to gradually become a strong global influence.

We shall learn from the history of Fujian on the Maritime Silk Road, explore the secret of success, seize the opportunity, stride into a new era with confidence, and create a victorious future.

Xie Bizhen

Preface

Fujian, located on the southeast coast of China, has been one of the important windows for economic, trade, and cultural exchanges between the East and the West since ancient times. Here, the Eastern and Western civilizations meet and blend again and again, rippling the river of time.

Fujian is home to many thriving ports, tidal lands, and islands. For a long time, it has been the center of China's foreign transportation, trade, and cultural exchanges. In the history of the Maritime Silk Road, Fujian has made brilliant achievements with its leading shipbuilding technology and seamanship, its unique natural and geographical advantages, its wealth of foreign trade products, and its trade spirit of bravery, perseverance, sincerity, and trustworthiness.

The contacts and exchanges between Fujian and Europe were mainly achieved through the rise of the Maritime Silk Road. The Port of Quanzhou was both the starting point and end point of the Maritime Silk Road. During the Song and Yuan Dynasties, the goods shipped from Quanzhou abroad were exported to the West. With the prosperity of the Maritime Silk Road, Westerners began to observe, understand and scrutinize the history of Fujian, which is the initial form of Fujian's economy and culture spreading to the West.

In the early Ming Dynasty, Zheng He's voyages to the West symbolized the prosperity of Fujian's maritime civilization. Fujian's world-leading shipbuilding technology was fully displayed during this period. Zheng He's strong fleet reflected Fujian's unparalleled shipbuilding level in those years; Fujianese excellent seamanship enabled them to be active in the sails. Zheng He's voyages to the West strengthened the economic, trade, political, and cultural exchanges between China and the countries along the Maritime Silk Road.

In the early Ming Dynasty, a ban on maritime trade or intercourse with foreign countries was enforced until Emperor Longqing briefly opened the sea. During this period, private maritime trade thrived. As the contact between Fujian and various Western forces deepened, Fujian culture spread worldwide. Meanwhile, Westerners were also very active in Fujian to examine and understand Fujian society more comprehensively and systematically.

Southern Fujian maritime merchants are a legendary group. For a long time in the late Ming and early Qing dynasties, they dominated Fujian's maritime foreign trade network and led the business in the southeastern seas. The Hokkien maritime business group, represented by the Zheng Chenggong family, has been in the waters of Fujian and Taiwan for decades. In its contact with Western colonial forces, it was never at a disadvantage, showing the solid maritime power of the people along the coast of Fujian.

During the Ming and Qing dynasties, missionaries traveled to China to preach their religions, elevating the cultural exchange between China and the West to a new peak. During this period, the multi-talented missionaries also introduced and reported relatively scattered natural and humanistic profiles of Fujian to the Western society from various aspects while Fujianese first began to emigrate to the West, conveying the essence and meaning of oriental culture to the Westerners.

In modern times, Fujian once again played the role of a bridge between East and West in economic, trade, and cultural exchanges. Chinese scholars who introduced Western ideas, and Fujian tea and porcelain, which are widely popular in the West, closely linked Fujian with the development of global modernization, making Fujian once again at the forefront of east-west transportation and cultural exchanges.

After the Opium War, a great flock of foreigners came to Fujian, and the door opened by Fujian society reflects the strong desire of the East and the West to understand and explore each other's culture. During this period, the eastward transmission of western sciences and the westward transmission of Fujianese culture were happening at an unprecedented height and speed on the track of two-way communication between Fujian and the West. They have greatly affected the historical progress of Fujian and the West. And the historical development they have contributed to is thought-provoking.

The history of contacts and exchanges between Fujian and the West is generally a two-way communication of equal exchanges and active dialogue. Despite the military conflicts and wars between China and the West, peace has always been the mainstream. Today, to rebuild the 21st Century Maritime Silk Road, we must continue to uphold our ancestors' boldness to embrace diversity, inherit their broad and profound wisdom, master advanced science and technology, and actively implement the strategy of politics, economy, and culture going abroad by relying on strong national hard power and cultural soft power. Based on friendly and equal exchanges with people of all ethnic groups in the world, we strive for mutual benefits, seek common ground while reserving differences, and make contributions to the general pattern of sustainable and peaceful development of the world and mankind.

Contents

CHAPTER 1

A Dim Beauty—Travelers, Oriental Voyages, and First Acquaintance of Fujian

The communication between the West and China dates back ages, and the contacts and exchanges between the West and Fujian also have a long history. From the Southern Song Dynasty to the Yuan Dynasty, its prosperity of commerce and trade attracted great interest from Westerners. With the help of the convenient seaways, some Westerners began to travel and inspect Fujian, leaving a wealth of records and knowledge about Fujian society. In that period, the interaction between the West and Fujian in the history of the Maritime Silk Road kicked off.

1 From *The City of Light* to *The Travels of Marco Polo*

In 1299, the Ottoman Empire was established. In its heyday, it crossed the Eurasian continent and controlled the arterial traffic connecting the east and west land transportation. Since this land transportation controlled by the Turks blocked the land passage from Europe to China, the Europeans had to turn to the sea and initially opened up a sea route to China. During the Song and Yuan dynasties, the maritime trade between Fujian and Europe began to rise.

The academic circle commonly believes that *The Travels of Marco Polo* is the beginning of Europeans traveling to China and their understanding of Fujian. This book is considered to be the first comprehensive introduction to the developed Chinese material civilization and spiritual civilization to Europeans. It records the author's experiences in various parts of China from 1275 to 1291, including Youxi, Fuzhou, Quanzhou, and other cities of

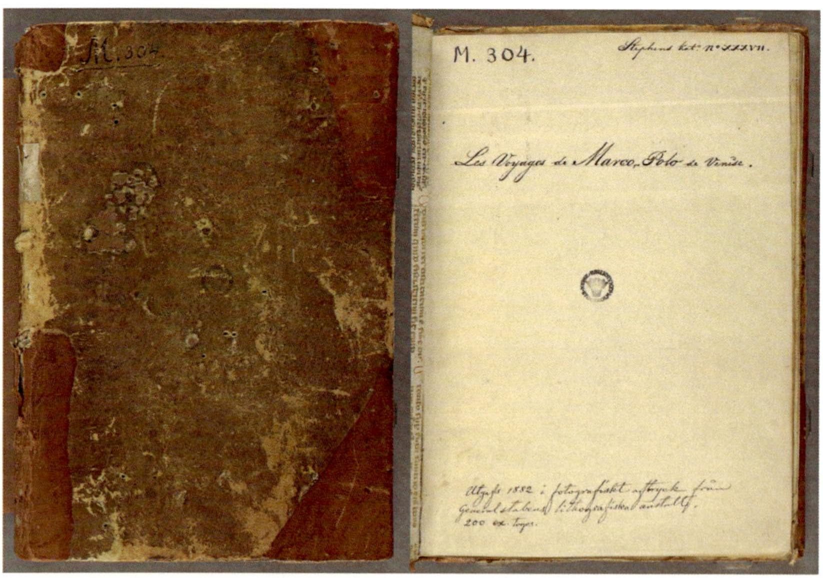

⦿ *The Travels of Marco Polo*, sample page

Fujian. In the eyes of Marco Polo, Fujian, which faces the sea, has the natural convenience to engage in overseas trade, and the Sino-foreign trade there was highly developed. He wrote Fuzhou and Quanzhou were the major ports for Sino-foreign trade at the time.

In recent years, the publication of the book *The City of Light* pushed forward the time when Westerners first knew China before Marco Polo. This travelogue mainly describes the legendary experience of Jacob d'Ancona, an Italian, who traveled to Quanzhou from Europe and did business in Quanzhou. It vividly depicts the prosperity of Quanzhou at the turn from the Song Dynasty to the Yuan Dynasty.

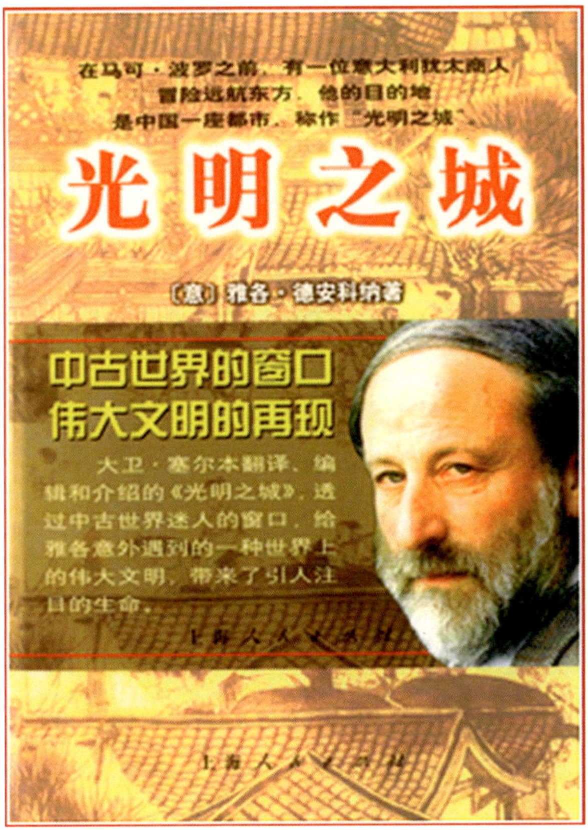

⦿ *The City of Light*, Chinese translation, sample page

2 Voyagers: Fujian in the Eyes of Franciscans

In the Yuan Dynasty, the Westerners who traveled to China and composed reports were not only travelers but also Catholic Franciscan missionaries who came to preach their religion. Western missionaries arrived in Fujian by sea. In addition to their missions or travels, they recorded their experiences and thoughts in China.

In 1313, Quanzhou of Fujian established a Catholic diocese, with Franciscans Gerard, Pofegrine of Castello, and Andrew of Perigia serving as bishops successively. They have left valuable written materials about Quanzhou's educational affairs and social conditions.

⊙ Tombstone of Bishop Andrew of Perigia

The missionary/traveler Odoric of Pordenone arrived in Guangzhou in 1321, passed through Quanzhou, Fuzhou, and Hangzhou, and traveled all the way north. He had a basic understanding of the Chinese social outlook. *The Travels of Friar Odoric*, compiled from his oral accounts, narrates his personal experiences, many of which are new content not covered by *The Travels of Marco Polo*.

Giovanni dei Marignolli was the last envoy sent by the Pope to China. He arrived in China in August 1342, and after he reached Quanzhou in about 1346, he boarded a ship and started his way home. During his stay in China, he toured around Quanzhou and later described his rough impression of Quanzhou in the book *The Travels of Marignolli*, which records his observations and experiences and confirms the development of the Franciscans in Quanzhou in the Yuan Dynasty.

⦿ *The Travels of Friar Odoric*, Chinese translation, sample page

3 Cross Lotus: The Spread of Christianity in Fujian in the Yuan Dynasty and Its Remains

The rulers of the Yuan Dynasty implemented a policy of tolerance for religious beliefs, and Christianity gained room for development in Fujian.

At the time, Christianity had two main factions in Quanzhou—Catholicism and Nestorianism. Many elements of the Christian style have been found on the tombstones of foreigners that still remain today, which fully demonstrates the wide spread of Christianity in Quanzhou during the Yuan Dynasty.

Correspondingly, the Yuan government also set up the Commission for the Promotion of Religion to manage Western religious activities and venues such as missionaries and churches.

The rise of Nestorianism in Quanzhou in the Yuan Dynasty had an important influence on Quanzhou society:

⊙ Yuan Dynasty Nestorian stone slab—Four-winged angel statue

⊙ Yuan Dynasty Nestorian Greek-style cross and ogive tombstone

⊙ Yuan Dynasty Nestorian Greek-style cross and ogive stone carving

⊙ Yuan Dynasty Nestorian cylindrical cross stone carving

⊙ Sumeru seat altar-style tombstone

Yuan Dynasty Christian tombstone

⊙ Yuan Dynasty Nestorian cross lotus tomb

⊙ Cross lotus angel inscription

It promoted the prosperity of commerce and trade in Quanzhou. The compatibility of different religions widely attracted businessmen from all over the world to gather in Quanzhou, making its foreign trade flourish.

It contributed to the cultural progress of Quanzhou and its prosperous joint development of multiculturism, which is an essential factor for the Chinese culture to maintain its vitality and sustainable development.

It propelled the growth of Quanzhou's foreign relations. The spread and development of Nestorianism there enhanced the friendly exchanges between Quanzhou and countries in Central Asia and West Asia. Also, they played a positive role in the peaceful development of human society.

It has left a precious legacy for the development of Quanzhou culture today.

Quanzhou was once the cultural capital of East Asia and a hot spot on the Maritime Silk Road. Historically, the social influence of Nestorianism in Quanzhou has been lasting to this day.

⦿ A facsimile of the Yuan Dynasty Nestorian cross slab unearthed in Quanzhou

CHAPTER 2

Pursuing Profits—Colonists, Cargos, and East-West Relations in the Age of Discovery

Since the 15th and 16th centuries, Westerners have ushered in the era of colonial expansion in the Age of Discovery. They opened up two sea routes to China, mainly developed and controlled by the Portuguese and Spaniards.

As an important area of the Maritime Silk Road, Fujian's abundant products and vast market have always been the source of profits for Westerners. The ban on maritime trade or intercourse with foreign countries in the Ming Dynasty stimulated the rise of private maritime trade. The distance between Fujian and the world has become narrower and narrower due to their frequent communication on the Maritime Silk Road.

1 Fujian and the Old Colonialist Countries

Westerners' desire for Fujian's goods stems from the profit-seeking drive of the global expansion of Western colonial powers in the Age of Discovery. Portugal was the first to open the eastern route. Portuguese sailed along the coast of Africa to the Indian Ocean, crossed the Strait of Malacca to Southeast Asia, reached the coastal areas of China, and connected with the overseas trade routes of Fujian.

⊙ Portuguese fleet

In 1517, a Portuguese fleet anchored in Zhangzhou. It was the first time the Portuguese sailed to Fujian and went ashore. While seeking trade, they also conducted comprehensive and in-depth reports on Fujian, the representative works of which are the *China Report* by Galeote Pereira and *Records of China* by Gasparda Cruz. These two books represented the high level of Westerners' understanding of China at that time and greatly enriched their understanding of Fujian and even Chinese society.

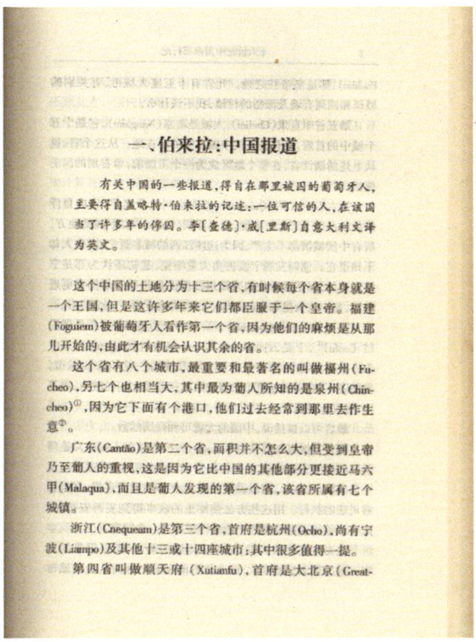

一、伯来拉：中国报道

有关中国的一些报道，得自在那里被囚的葡萄牙人，主要得自盖略特·伯来拉的记述：一位可信的人，在该国当了许多年的俘囚。李[查德]·威[里斯]自意大利文译为英文。

这个中国的土地分为十三个省，有时候每个省本身就是一个王国，但是这许多年来它们都臣服于一个皇帝。福建(Foguiem)被葡萄牙人看作第一个省，因为他们的麻烦是从那儿开始的，由此才有机会认识其余的省。

这个省有八个城市，最重要和最著名的叫做福州(Fucheo)，另七个也相当大，其中最为葡人所知的是泉州(Chincheo)①，因为它下面有个港口，他们过去经常到那里去作生意②。

广东(Cantão)是第二个省，面积并不怎么大，但受到皇帝乃至葡人的重视，这是因为它比中国的其他部分更接近马六甲(Malaqua)，而且是葡人发现的第一个省，该省所属有七个城镇。

浙江(Cnequeam)是第三个省，首府是杭州(Ocho)，尚有宁波(Liampo)及其他十三或十四座城市；其中很多值得一提。

第四省叫做顺天府(Xutianfu)，首府是大北京(Great-

Galeote Pereira: *China Report*, Chinese translation, sample page

Spain tagged Portugal, opened up the Europe-America-Philippines-China trans-Pacific route, and occupied the Philippines, which it tried to use as a springboard to build relations with China.

In 1575, the Spanish missionary Martín De Rada of Order of Saint Augustine was ordered to lead a diplomatic corps to Fujian. During his stay in Fujian, Rada purchased over 100 Chinese books from Fujian, based on which he wrote two reports, *Records of the Mission to Fujian* and *Record of Events in Ming China*. These reports became an important source of information for westerners to understand China at that time and strengthened the exchange of Eastern and Western cultures.

⦿ Portrait of Rada

⦿ Manila carrack

2 Southern Fujian Maritime Merchants and Emerging Capitalist Countries

The Netherlands was an emerging capitalist country after Portugal and Spain. As the most powerful maritime hegemon in the world in the 17th century, it was nicknamed the "sea coachman."

In 1602, the Netherlands founded the East India Company to develop trade with the East. According to relevant materials, during the 80 years from 1602 to 1682, Dutch merchant ships sold 16 million pieces of Chinese porcelain, including blue and white porcelain from Zhangzhou and white porcelain from Dehua.

⦿ Headquarters of the Dutch East India Company in Amsterdam, now a school building of the University of Amsterdam

⦿ Dutch East India Company ships

⦿ Dutch trade ship

In 1622, the Dutch East India Company built a castle in Penghu as a trading base. In September 1624, the Dutch left Penghu for Taiwan. During the Dutch occupation of Taiwan, Japanese merchant ships sailed to Taiwan every year to buy deerskins and sell raw silk. The Dutch made enormous profits in the transit trade.

The Dutch were mainly active in the southeastern coastal areas and had close ties with the Hokkien maritime business group represented by the Zheng Chenggong family. After the Zheng family surrendered to the Qing government in 1683, the Dutch gradually faded out of the Chinese waters.

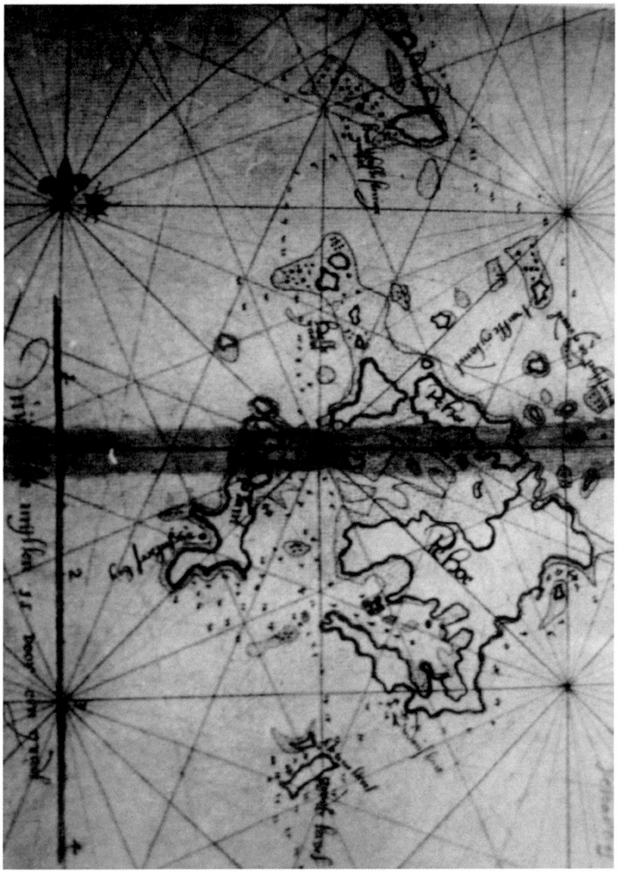

◉ 17th-century map of Penghu in the National Archives of the Netherlands

Fuzhou map drawn by the Dutch

⊙ Taiwanese Church in Dutch Ancient Books

⊙ The map of Fuzhou Bay drawn by the Dutch in the 18th century, including the islands from Fuzhou to the estuary of the Min River and Luoyuan Bay.

Britain was the emerging capitalist country that developed rapidly after the Netherlands. When the Netherlands was expelled from Taiwan in 1662, the British took the opportunity to establish trade relations with the Zheng family group and set up factories in Xiamen, Fuzhou, and Guangzhou, one after another, which turned out rather profitable. Then, as the Qing government's self-seclusion policy became stricter, the British trade in the Fujian waters gradually declined, too.

During the foreign trade along the coast of Fujian, Britain also made great efforts to investigate plants in Fujian. It was the first large-scale exploration and collection of natural products in China by Westerners, which greatly enriched the Western plant taxonomy.

⦿ British fleet

Tea specimens investigated by the British

Chinese tallow tree seed specimen

3 An Abundance of Wonderful Goods: Fujian and Western Commodities in European Trade Routes to East Asia

In the history of trade between the East and the West through the Maritime Silk Road, the circulation of commodities and the exchange of currency have always been the theme of the times. Commodities connected people of the two worlds from different regions, dramatically accelerating the development of global integration and the advancement of modern industrialization.

Porcelain

Fujian is an important base for the manufacture of Chinese ceramics. In a way, in history, it bore the critical mission of ceramic trade between the East and the West and bridged the business exchanges between the two worlds.

⊙ Bluish white glazed floral plate made in Yi kiln of Minqing County in the Song Dynasty

⊙ Dual-ear incense burner animal head ornament made in Dehua kiln

⊙ White glazed printed four-ear jar made in Dehua kiln

⊙ (LEFT) Elephant leg bottle made in Cizao kiln

⊙ (BELOW) Brown glazed four-ear jar made in Cizao kiln

⊙ Green glazed floral Plate made in Cizao kiln

⊙ Marco Polo incense burner, Dehua white porcelain, a common incense burner in Europe before the 17th century

Fujian ceramics manufacturing has a relatively long history. As early as the Sui, Tang, and Five Dynasties, Fujian pottery was exported to foreign countries. During the Song and Yuan Dynasties, Fujian ceramic culture experienced great development. The blue and white porcelain represented by those made in the Dehua kiln became an important commodity that sold goods at home and abroad. During the Ming and Qing Dynasties, the production of Fujian porcelain showed the regional cultural symbols and characteristics of Fujian porcelain craftsmanship. At that time, Dehua white porcelain and Clark blue and white porcelain sold like wildfire at home and abroad.

⦿ Clark Porcelain in Europe

Fujian blue and white porcelain export has substantially impacted Western European countries. It promoted improving material life and cultural taste, cultural integration and technological development, and international trade and navigation technology development in Western countries.

⊙ Blue and White Porcelain Exported from Fujian—Porcelain kettles with a dragon mouth

⊙ Blue and White Porcelain Exported from Fujian—Porcelain plates printed with European castles

⊙ Blue and white porcelain plate exported from Fujian

⦿ Blue and white porcelain beer mug exported from Fujian

⦿ (ABOVE) Blue and white porcelain bowls exported from Fujian

⦿ (RIGHT) Blue and White Porcelain Exported from Fujian—Porcelain plate printed with Mongolian soldiers

Tea

China is the origin of tea planting in the world, and high-quality tea species are mainly concentrated in the southeast region, especially Fujian tea, which is famous at home and abroad. During the Ming and Qing dynasties, tea gradually developed into one of the most important commodities in the maritime trade between the East and the West.

In the early 17th century, Dutch and British merchant ships that sailed to the far east transported the first batch of Fujian tea to Europe. After the 1620s, the European tea market expanded significantly, encouraging the large-scale cultivation, processing, and export of export-oriented tea in Fujian. The Dutch and British East India Companies were the leading tea suppliers in the European tea market then. They purchased tea from the southeastern coastal areas of China and sold it on the European continent to meet the tea consumption needs of Europeans.

⦿ Simulation diagram of tea planting, production, and process flow

In the 18th and 19th centuries, the remains of tea found on the sunk merchant ships of some Western countries are the historical imprint of the fact that tea bridged the trade between the East and the West since the Age of Discovery.

Simulated diagram of a tea shop

Fujian tea samples salvaged from shipwrecks in maritime trade

Silk

The Fujian textile industry has a long history, too. During the Northern Song Dynasty, Fujian became one of the important places that produced silk in China for a very brief time. Quanzhou grew into a world-renowned international trade port during the Song and Yuan Dynasties. Trade demands and the living needs of dignitaries deeply stimulated the development of Quanzhou's silk industry. Historical books and unearthed cultural relics provide valuable information for people to understand ancient Fujian society's silk industry and silk products.

⦿ The simulated diagram of raw silk preparation

⦿ Raw silk sample

Since the 16th century, as European ships sailed to the southeastern waters of China and established full connections with private merchant ships in southeast China, Fujian silk products gradually flowed from the traditional markets along the sea route to the sides of the Atlantic Ocean. The Maritime Silk Road trade route extended into a broader maritime trade network.

For example, when Hokkien maritime merchants traded silk with the Spaniards, the trade commodities, including silk, acquired by the Hokkien maritime merchants from the coastal areas of Fujian, Jiangsu, and Zhejiang became the primary source of goods for the trans-Pacific trade of the Manila carracks steered by the Spaniards. Since the Qing Dynasty, the share of silk fabrics in the maritime trade between China and the West was gradually inferior to tea. Still, until the Opium War, raw silk remained an essential cargo transported by ships to the West.

⊙ Silk fabrics

⊙ Satin loom

Silver dollar

With the Manila carracks, the Spaniards transported a wealth of silver dollars from South America to the Philippines every year to purchase Chinese goods from Fujian maritime merchants. As a result, many Spanish and other types of silver dollars poured into Fujian, as evidenced by many historical records and archaeological discoveries.

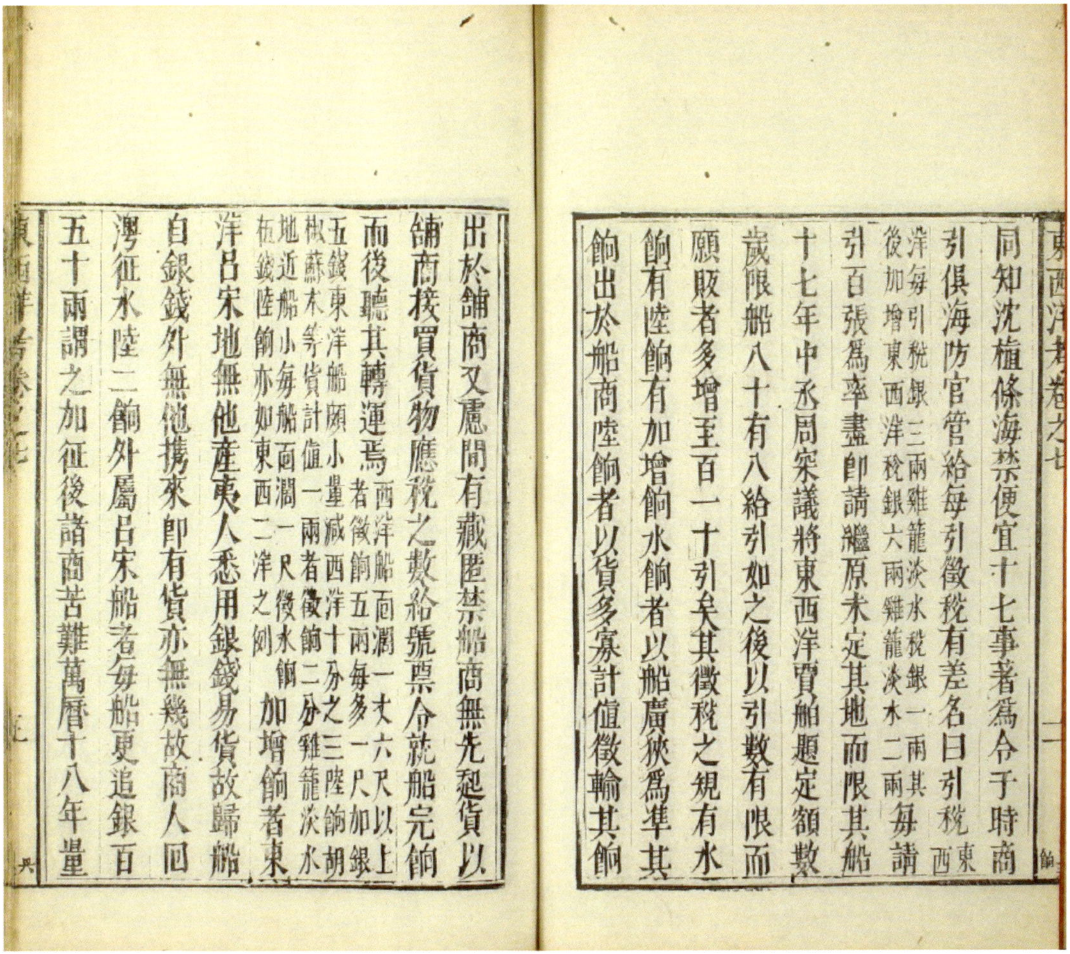

同知沈植條海禁便宜十七事著爲令于時商
引俱海防官管給每引徵税有差名曰引税（東西洋每引税銀三兩雞籠淡水税銀一兩其後加增東西洋税銀六兩雞籠淡水二兩）每請
引百張爲率盡即請繼原未定其地而限其船
十七年中丞周寀議將東西洋貿船題定額數
歲限船八十有八給引如之後以引數有限而
願販者多增至百一十引矣其徵税之規有水
餉有陸餉有加增餉水餉者以船廣狹爲準其
餉出於船商陸餉者以貨多寡計值徵輸其餉

出於鋪商又慮間有藏匿禁船商無先起貨以
鋪商接買貨物應税之數給號票令就船完餉
而後聽其轉運焉（西洋船面濶一丈六尺以上者徵餉五兩每多一尺加銀五錢東洋船頗小量減西洋十分之三陸餉胡椒蘇木等貨計值一兩者徵餉二分雞籠淡水地近船小每船面濶一尺徵水餉五錢陸餉亦如東西二洋之例）加增餉者東
洋呂宋地無他產夷人悉用銀錢易貨故歸船
自銀錢外無他携來即有貨亦無幾故商人回
澳征水陸二餉外屬呂宋船者每船更追銀百
五十兩謂之加征後諸商苦難萬曆十八年量

⦿ *Research on Eastern and Western Oceans*, sample page

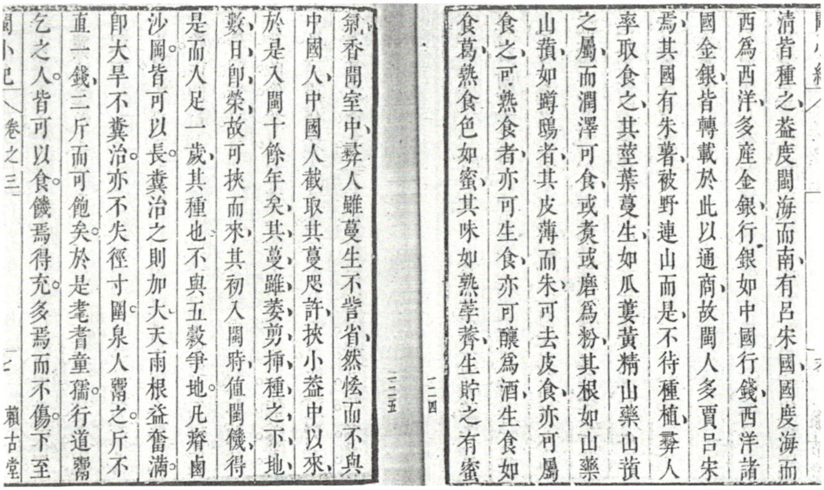

清皆種之。蓋度閩海而南有呂宋國，國度海而西為西洋，多產金銀，行銀如中國行錢。西洋諸國金銀，皆轉載於此以通商，故閩人多賈呂宋焉。其國有朱薯，被野連山而是，不待種植，彝人率取食之。其莖葉蔓生，如瓜蔞、黃精、山藥、山蕷之屬，而潤澤可食，或煮或磨為粉。其根如山藥、山蕷，如蹲鴟者，其皮薄而朱，可去皮食，亦可屬食之，可熟食者，亦可生食，亦可釀為酒。生食如食葛，熟食色如蜜，其味如熟荸薺，生貯之有蜜

一二四

氣，香聞室中。彝人雖蔓生不訾省，然恡而不與中國人，中國人截取其蔓咫許，挾小蓋中以來，於是入閩十餘年矣。其蔓雖萎，剪插種之，下地數日即榮，故可挾而來。其初入閩，時值閩饑，得是而人足一歲。其種也，不與五穀爭地，凡瘠鹵沙岡皆可以長。糞治之則加大，天雨根益奮滿。即大旱不糞治，亦不失徑寸圍。泉人鬻之，斤不直一錢，二斤而可飽矣。於是耄耆童孺，行道鬻乞之人，皆可以食。饑焉得充，多焉而不傷。下至

一二五

閩小紀／卷之三　賴古堂

⦿ *Records of Min*, sample page

⦿ Dutch gold coins

⦿ Dutch East India Company copper coin

⦿ Dutch Sphinx silver coin (1576)

⦿ Silver coin with the portrait of Spanish Mexico Carlos IV

⊙ Spanish silver coins

⊙ Spanish silver coin (peseta)

CHAPTER 3

Battles at Sea—Sino-West Naval Battles and Military Conflicts in the Waters of Fujian and Taiwan

When opening up the sea route to East Asia and the Chinese market, the Europeans did not always wear a peaceful and friendly face. They often adopted violent means. Western powers successfully launched colonial aggression on both Fujian and Taiwan, pushing Fujian to the frontline of resisting overseas aggression, and involved it in the development course of world marine history.

1 Swords Crossed—The Armed Intrusion of Western Colonists and the Conflict between China and the West

In opening up the global market, the western colonists were backed up by strong maritime armed forces to prevent the harassment of pirates and the restriction of trading countries. Therefore, the commercial history of maritime trade between the West and China is also a history of wars and conflicts between naval powers.

Sailing equipment of western colonists

When the Europeans expanded eastwards in the Age of Discovery, strong ships and weapons enabled them to dominate the sea. Portugal and Britain had standing navies in the 15th and 16th centuries, and the Portuguese fleet's footprint spread throughout the eastern hemisphere because of its strong shipbuilding capabilities and technology.

⦿ Portuguese warship model

The Portuguese sailboats, capable of commerce and combat, were impressively powerful on the route to Asia. This kind of sailboat was an improved multi-masted sailboat, thus suitable as a frigate or to undertake coast guard tasks. It was called the first batch of ocean-going vessels specially developed for maritime combat of the European navies.

In the naval reforms of Western Europe in the 15th and 16th centuries, expanding the use of ship-based artillery was equally important as improving management. In the 13th century, the prototype of artillery had been made, but it was not used effectively in naval battles. In the 15th and 16th centuries, Western European countries successively equipped heavy artillery on their ocean-going vessels, which continued to be improved, and enhanced the power of their warships.

⦿ Dutch warship

⦿ Galley warships of Venice

⦿ British squadron warship in Late Qing Dynasty

⊙ Nautical weaponry—Western artillery

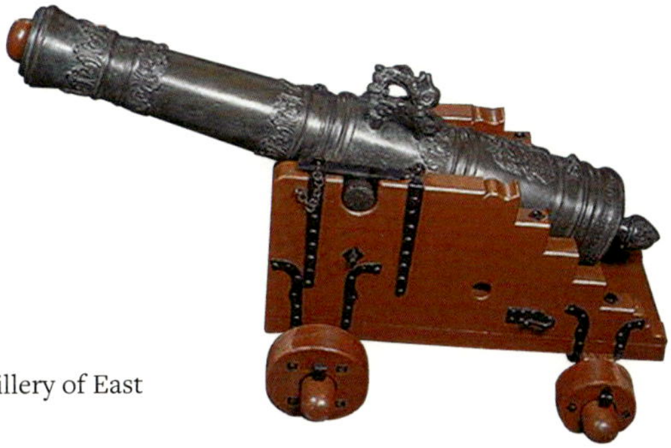

⊙ Nautical weaponry—Western Artillery of East India Company

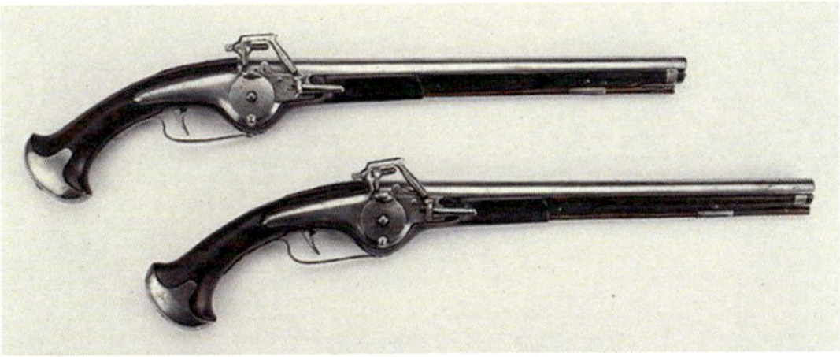

⊙ Nautical weaponry—Sidearms

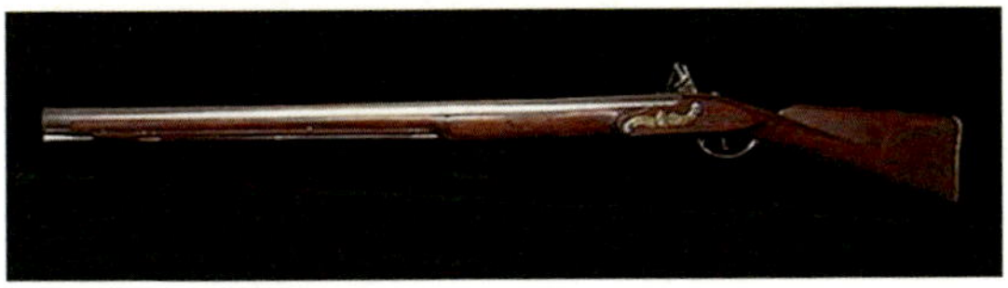

⊙ Nautical weaponry—Rifles

⊙ Nautical weaponry—Helmets

⦿ Portuguese sailors who went ashore and surveyed during the Age of Discovery (16th century)

⦿ Dutch sailors/soldiers in Taiwan in the 17th century

The advancement of nautical instruments and seamanship was necessary for Europeans' expansion to the eastern seas. In the 13th century, nautical instruments became increasingly popular in Europe. Especially after the compass was used, Europeans applied the magnetic needle to maritime activities. At the same time, nautical charts have also been developed accordingly. The astrolabe invented by the Portuguese in 1481 was widely used because it was lighter and simpler. As time went by, the nautical instruments were developed and enriched, and the square (late 15th century), Davis backstaff (late 16th century), octant (1730), and sextant (1759) appeared successively.

⊙ European nautical instrument—Quadrant

⊙ European nautical instrument—Astrolabe

⊙ European nautical instrument—Telescope, compass, etc.

⦿ European nautical instrument—Sextant

⦿ European nautical instrument—Compass

The Battle of Zoumaxi

⦿ Portrait of Zhu Wan

Since 1523, the Ming government-enforced ban on maritime trade or intercourse with foreign countries, which halted lawful overseas trade. After that, Western colonial forces invaded China's southeastern coastal areas and widely engaged in pirate trade with private maritime groups, triggering a crisis in the coastal defense and social and economic development of China's southeastern sea frontier.

In 1548, Zhu Wan launched the Battle of Shuangyu, which wiped out the Japanese pirates and Portuguese on the island of Shuangyu. In 1549, Portuguese and pirate ships anchored in the Zoumaxi area of Zhao'an Bay invaded and looted the surrounding villages. Later, Zhu Wan led an army to destroy them, and the Portuguese forces disappeared in the seas off. This battle was an important naval battle against Western colonialists in the Ming Dynasty, which deserves to be remembered forever.

⦿ Zoumaxi Harbor (present-day)

⊙ Model of Fujian Naval Warship in Ming Dynasty

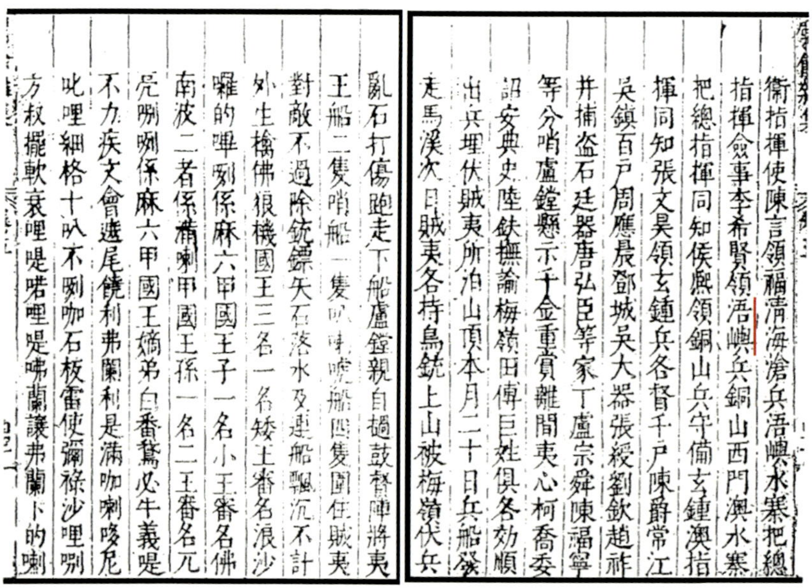

衛指揮使陳言領福清海滄兵浯嶼水寨把總
指揮僉事李希賢領浯嶼兵銅山西門澳水寨
把總指揮同知侯熙領銅山兵守備玄鍾澳指
揮同知張文昊領玄鍾兵各督千戶陳爵常江
兵鎮百戶周應晨鄧城吳大器張綬劉欽趙祚
并捕盜石廷器唐弘臣等家丁盧宗舜陳福寧
等分哨盧鏜懸示千金重賞離間夷心柯喬委
詔安典史陸鈇撫諭梅嶺田傅巨姓俱各効順
出兵埋伏賊夷所泊山頂本月二十日兵船發
走馬溪次日賊夷各持鳥銃上山被梅嶺伏兵
亂石打傷跑走下船盧鏜親自擂鼓督陣將夷
王船二隻哨船一隻叭喇唬船四隻圍住賊夷
對敵不過除銃鏢矢石落水及連船飄沉不計
外生擒佛狼機國王三名一名矮王賽名浪沙
囉的嗶唎係麻六甲國王子一名小王賽名佛
南波二者係滿喇甲國王孫一名二王賽名兀
亮咧唦係麻六甲國王嫡弟白番鴛必牛義是
不力疾文會遜尾鐃利弗蘭利是滿咖喇哆尼
叱哩細格十叭不唎咖石板雷使彌祿沙哩唎
方叔擺軟哀哩哫啫哩哫咈蘭讓弗蘭卜的喇

⊙ Records of the Battle of Zoumaxi in *Pi Yu Za Ji* in the Ming Dynasty

Western forces invaded Moon Port

One of the most direct manifestations of the Western colonists' armed destruction is the invasion and plunder of the Moon Port in Zhangzhou.

After 1627, due to the tyranny of local government and the intrusion of Western colonists and overseas private armed forces, Moon Port went from flourishing to decadence. *The Zeelandia Diaries* written by the Dutch records in detail the situations where the Dutch carried out armed smuggling and looted Chinese ships in the Moon Port area from 1629 to 1655. It profoundly reflects the conflicts between Chinese and Western maritime forces in the waters of Fujian and Taiwan.

⊙ Old wharf of Moon Port

⦿ (LEFT) *The Zeelandia Diaries*, Chinese translation, sample page

⦿ (BELOW) Dutch ships operating along the coast of Fujian in the late Ming Dynasty

The Dutch East India Company invaded the coast of Fujian and Taiwan

Memorable Description of the East Indian Voyage, written by Willem Bontekoe, was one of the bestsellers in the 17th century in the Netherlands. Bontekoe recorded the Dutch East India Company's invasion and harassment of Taiwan and Fujian with his personal experience, which makes up for the absence of records in Chinese history annals. It disclosed the colonialist acts to the world with fair facts and provided scattered information about Taiwan and Fujian. In addition, the book contains sporadic accounts of Chinese naval and civilian resistance to the Dutch invasion and negotiations between Dutch and Qing officials.

⦿ *Memorable Description of the East Indian Voyage*, Chinese translation, cover

⦿ The Dutch invasion of the coast of Fujian

2 Southeast Lock—The Fight for Taiwan between the Netherlands and the Zheng Army

As the gateway to the southeast of China, Taiwan is nicknamed "the lock of the southeast, the fence of the seven provinces." And the Dutch naturally craved this coastal fortress, with such a critical strategic position and abundant resources, which could supply trade goods and a resting venue for Western colonists.

After the Dutch failed to occupy Penghu for the first time in 1604, they made another attempt to land on Penghu on July 11, 1622. In September 1624, intimidated by the strong Ming Dynasty army, the Dutch fleet left Penghu and retreated to Taiwan. After that, the Dutch started their long-term colonial rule of Taiwan.

In 1662, based on a series of victories in the earlier war against the Netherlands, Zheng Chenggong's army defeated the Dutch defenders in one swoop. The Dutch Governor of Taiwan, Frederick Coyett, signed the surrender agreement, declaring the end of the Dutch colonial rule in Taiwan. The military victory of Zheng Chenggong's army in Taiwan has dealt a massive blow to foreign colonial aggression forces and defended the territorial integrity of China.

⦿ Portrait of Frederick Coyett

⊙ Zheng Chenggong's fleet engaged in a naval battle with Dutch ships off the coast of Taiwan

⊙ The Dutch defenders of Provintia (now Chikan City) surrendered to Zheng Chenggong

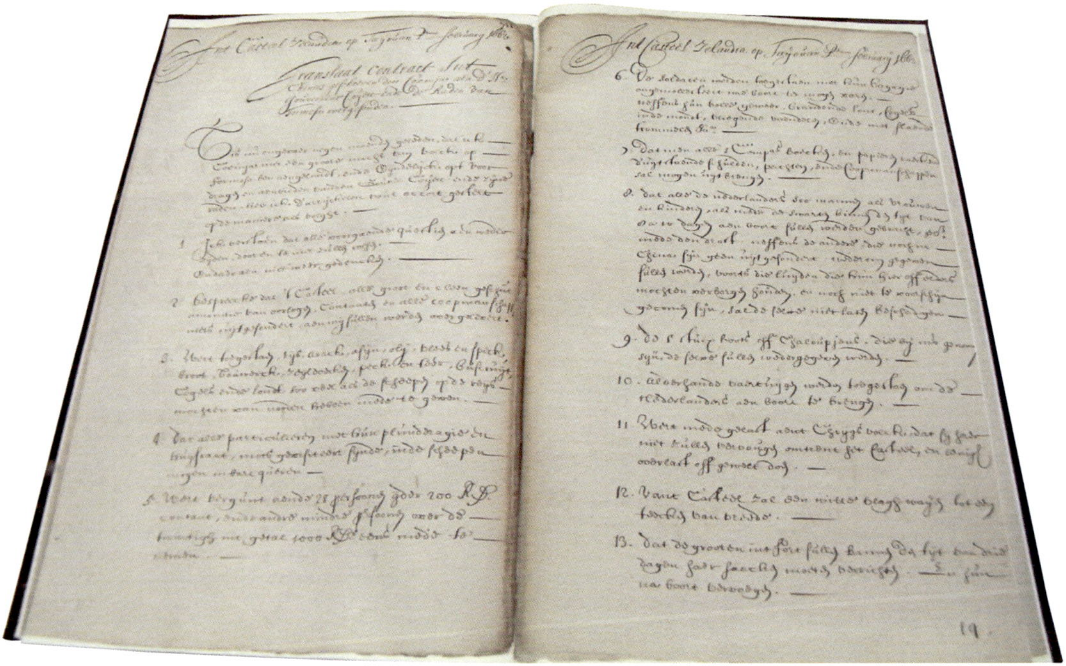

⊙ The agreement between the Dutch and the Zheng Army

3 Crisis of China—The British Invasion of the Coast of Fujian

Following the Netherlands, Britain gradually prospered and became the world's number one capitalist power. It also actively expanded eastward, opening up colonies, plundering raw materials, and dumping British goods. The British intrusion and invasion along the coast of Fujian and Taiwan were an essential part of the modern Opium War.

Before the Opium War, the British invaders sent spies to investigate the southeastern coastal areas of China. German missionary Charles Gutzlaf visited China's coast thrice from 1831 to 1833, collecting intelligence about Xiamen, Fuzhou, Fujian, and China's inland areas, which provided information for the British colonial army to invade China in the future. When the investigation finished, Gutzlaf compiled the records of his three voyages into a book, *Three Voyages along the Coast of China in 1831, 1832, 1833*, which provided information for Westerners to understand China at that time.

⦿ Portrait of Charles Gutzlaf

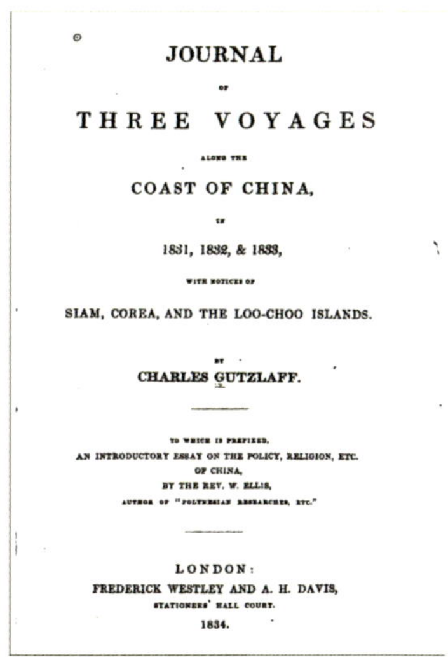

JOURNAL

OF

THREE VOYAGES

ALONG THE

COAST OF CHINA,

IN

1831, 1832, & 1833,

WITH NOTICES OF

SIAM, COREA, AND THE LOO-CHOO ISLANDS.

BY

CHARLES GUTZLAFF.

TO WHICH IS PREFIXED,
AN INTRODUCTORY ESSAY ON THE POLICY, RELIGION, ETC.
OF CHINA,
BY THE REV. W. ELLIS,
AUTHOR OF "POLYNESIAN RESEARCHES, ETC."

LONDON:
FREDERICK WESTLEY AND A. H. DAVIS,
STATIONERS' HALL COURT.
1834.

⦿ Journal of Three Voyages along the Coast of China in 1831, 1832, & 1833

To reverse the trade deficit with China, the British continued to smuggle a large amount of opium into the Chinese market, which brought a serious disaster and crisis to Chinese society. As a frontline position along the coast, Fujian Province was also an important spot for opium smuggling and circulation at that time. Justus Doolittle, an American missionary living in Fuzhou at the time, described that there were more opium dens than rice shops, which shows the rampancy of opium.

Lin Zexu, a famous anti-opium pioneer and national hero, was a native of Fuzhou. Having witnessed the rampant opium smoking in his hometown, he detested it and made up his mind to ban opium, which eventually led to the destruction of opium at Humen.

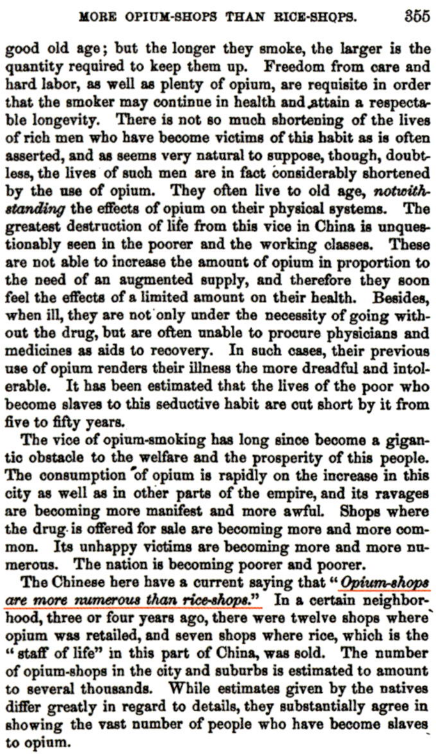

MORE OPIUM-SHOPS THAN RICE-SHOPS. 355

good old age; but the longer they smoke, the larger is the quantity required to keep them up. Freedom from care and hard labor, as well as plenty of opium, are requisite in order that the smoker may continue in health and attain a respectable longevity. There is not so much shortening of the lives of rich men who have become victims of this habit as is often asserted, and as seems very natural to suppose, though, doubtless, the lives of such men are in fact considerably shortened by the use of opium. They often live to old age, *notwithstanding* the effects of opium on their physical systems. The greatest destruction of life from this vice in China is unquestionably seen in the poorer and the working classes. These are not able to increase the amount of opium in proportion to the need of an augmented supply, and therefore they soon feel the effects of a limited amount on their health. Besides, when ill, they are not only under the necessity of going without the drug, but are often unable to procure physicians and medicines as aids to recovery. In such cases, their previous use of opium renders their illness the more dreadful and intolerable. It has been estimated that the lives of the poor who become slaves to this seductive habit are cut short by it from five to fifty years.

The vice of opium-smoking has long since become a gigantic obstacle to the welfare and the prosperity of this people. The consumption of opium is rapidly on the increase in this city as well as in other parts of the empire, and its ravages are becoming more manifest and more awful. Shops where the drug is offered for sale are becoming more and more common. Its unhappy victims are becoming more and more numerous. The nation is becoming poorer and poorer.

The Chinese here have a current saying that "*Opium-shops are more numerous than rice-shops.*" In a certain neighborhood, three or four years ago, there were twelve shops where opium was retailed, and seven shops where rice, which is the "staff of life" in this part of China, was sold. The number of opium-shops in the city and suburbs is estimated to amount to several thousands. While estimates given by the natives differ greatly in regard to details, they substantially agree in showing the vast number of people who have become slaves to opium.

◉ The phenomenon that Fuzhou opium dens outnumbered rice shops recorded in the writings of modern Westerners

◉ Portrait of Lin Zexu

Deng Tingzhen (1776–1846) assisted Lin in banning opium and repelling the provocation of British ships. In July 1840, the British ships invaded Xiamen, and Deng personally led the navy to repel the invading army. After the outbreak of the Opium War, the British army encountered brave resistance in the Guangzhou area and turned to Xiamen. As Deng had added and repaired the fortresses, purchased and cast new cannons, and strengthened the navy in advance, the British army's attempt to invade Xiamen failed, and it had to go north along the coast.

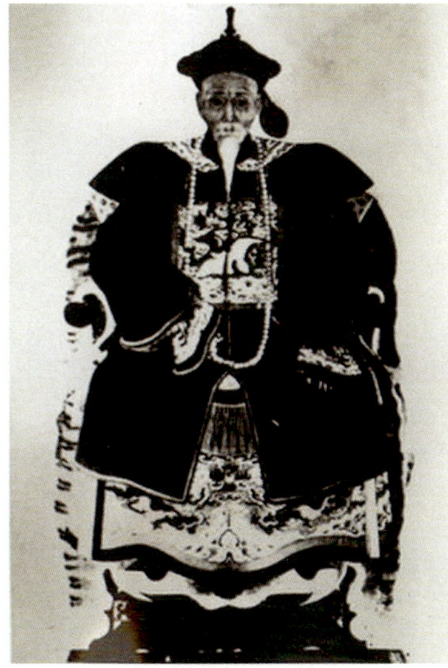

⦿ Portrait of Deng Tingzhen

⦿ Hulishan Fortress in Xiamen

From August 1841 to June 1842, the British invaders expanded the scope of the war to the coastal areas of Fujian and Zhejiang. They forcibly occupied Xiamen, Dinghai, Zhenhai, Ningbo, and Zhapu one after another. In the resistance against the British invaders' invasion of Xiamen, the Fujian military and civilians were well prepared and dealt the invaders a heavy blow. Unfortunately, due to the improper command of the primary decision-maker and the inferior military strength, Xiamen was occupied at last.

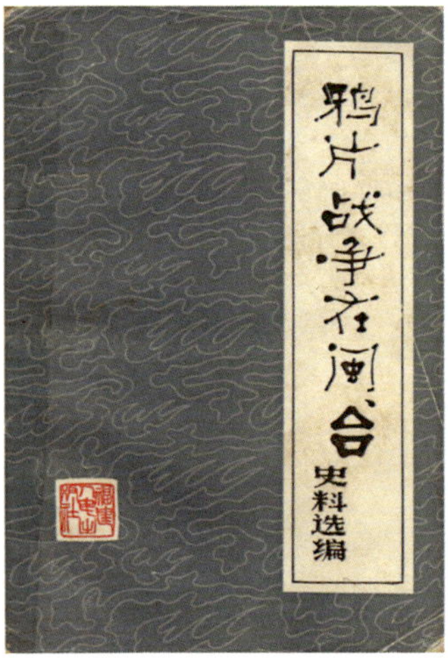

⦿ (LEFT) *Selected History of the Opium War in Fujian and Taiwan*, cover

⦿ (BELOW) In August 1841, British warships attacked Xiamen

After Xiamen fell, people in the urban area and villages voluntarily united to fight heroically against the invaders. At that time, though the British invaders occupied Xiamen, they did not dare to stay in the urban area for long, believing that it was unwise to venture into the city. In September 1841, the British fleet withdrew from Xiamen.

⦿ Xiamen soldiers and civilians bravely resisted the British invaders

When Western powers invaded China's southeast coast, Taiwan, which is a strategically important place, always bore the brunt of the intrusion. Britain showed interest in Taiwan long ago. It set up a business office in Taiwan in the second half of the 17th century, but as the Qing China recovered Taiwan, the British aggression against Taiwan had to stop. In the early stage of the Opium War, British opium dealers had clamored to occupy some islands off the coast of China, but during the Opium War, all five invasions of Taiwan by Britain failed.

Yao Ying (1785–1853), born in Tongcheng, Anhui, was an officer deployed to manage Taiwan when the Opium War broke out. He worked with Dahong'a to defend Taiwan. After the war broke out, Yao petitioned the Qing government for permission to hire civilians to form the navy from Penghu and build warships in Xiamen. Under his overall planning and efficient leadership, Taiwan's soldiers and civilians were well prepared for war, which created a strong defense for Taiwan then, and made the British aggressors suffer.

Dahong'a (?–1854), a native of Manchuria with Bordered Yellow Banners, was a famous general who led the Taiwanese military and civilians to resist the British invasion during the Opium War. In 1835, he was appointed as the commander-in-chief of Taiwan. After the outbreak of the Opium War, he organized the Taiwanese military and civilians to repel multiple attacks by the British invaders, killed and captured hundreds of British soldiers and defeated them again and again. The Taiwan battlefield was the only place where the Qing government had achieved victory during the Opium War.

⦿ Portrait of Yao Ying

⦿ Portrait of Dahong'a

After the *Treaty of Nanjing* was signed, China was forced to open itself, and Chinese society became increasingly involved in the global market expanded by Western capitalism. In the history of the Maritime Silk Road and East-West trade, China was put in a passive position. As required in the *Treaty of Nanjing*, Fujian was forced to open the two trading ports of Xiamen and Fuzhou, which shows that Westerners attached great importance to this huge Fujian market. From then on, the coastal areas of Fujian have gradually embarked on the road of modernization.

⊙ The signing of the *Treaty of Nanjing*

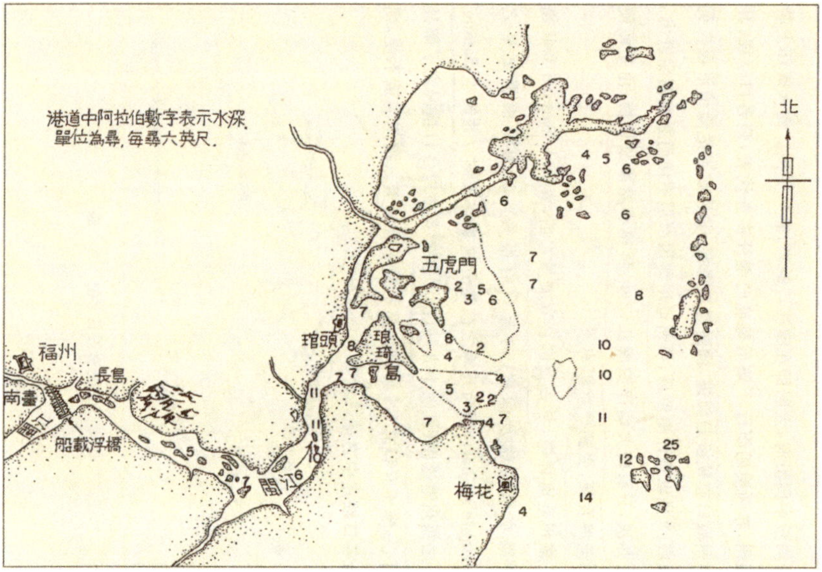

⦿ Map of Fuzhou Port in the Late Qing Dynasty

⦿ Overview of Xiamen Island and Gulangyu Island under the lens of Westerners in the Late Qing Dynasty

CHAPTER 4

The Liturgical Dispute—The Exchange and Collision of Fujian and Western Cultures During the Ming and Qing Dynasties

As the main artery of the ancient East-West trade and transportation, the Maritime Silk Road not only bridged the interaction between the East and the West in terms of geographical transportation, commodity trade, and political and military activities but also shouldered the mission of cultural exchange between China and the West. It has promoted the exchange and collision of the two major civilized worlds.

1 *A Dialogue on God as the Creator and Governor of the Universe* (*San Shan Lun Xue*)—"the Western Confucius," Stories of Giulio Aleni in Fujian

Giulio Aleni (1582–1649), following Matteo Ricci, is another famous Jesuit in the history of communications between China and the West. Having made outstanding contributions to cultural exchanges between China and the west, he earned the nickname the "Western Confucius" among Chinese literati and officials.

⦿ Portrait of Giulio Aleni

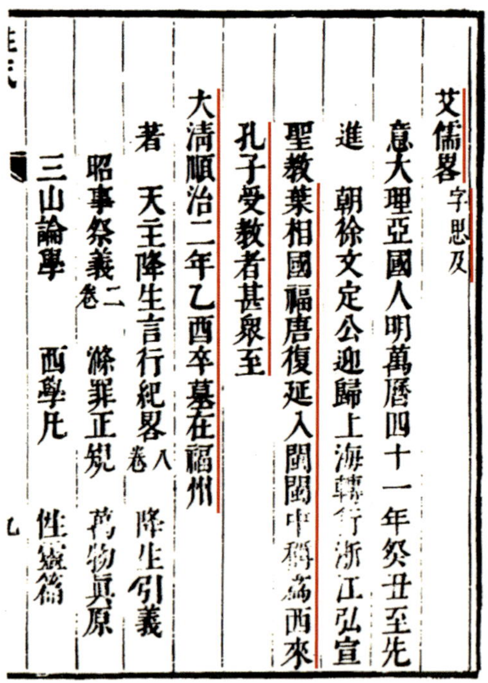

艾儒畧 字思及
意大理亞國人明萬曆四十一年癸丑至先
進 朝徐文定公迎歸上海轉行浙江弘宣
聖教葉相國福唐復延入閩閩中稱為西來
孔子受教者甚衆至
大清順治二年乙酉卒墓在福州
著 天主降生言行紀畧八卷 降生引義
昭事祭義二卷 滌罪正規 萬物眞原
三山論學 西學凡 性靈篇

⦿ Chinese literati and officialdom praised Giulio Aleni as the Western Confucius

⦿ Portrait of Ye Xianggao

In 1610, Aleni entered China as a missionary and preached in Beijing, Shanghai, Yangzhou, Kaifeng, Hangzhou, etc. In 1624, Aleni came to Fuzhou with Ye Xianggao, a native of Fujian, and started to spread Catholicism in Fujian in the late Ming and early Qing dynasties, thus building an indissoluble bond with Fujian.

When Aleni preached in Fujian, he paid great heed to combine the dissemination of Western knowledge with the propagation of Catholic doctrines. He tried to open the hearts of the Chinese people with this Western knowledge of science and technology. He compiled and published dozens of works. In the aspect of propagating Western knowledge, his representative works are *Complete Map of the Myriad Countries*, *Kun Yu Tu Shuo*, *Zhi Fang Wai Ji*, *Xi Fang Da Wen*, *Xi Xue Fan*, *Ji Xue Yao Fa*, and others. These works opened a window for the Fujian literati, officials, and Chinese intellectuals to understand Western science and social culture.

⦿ *Xi Fang Da Wen*, sample page

⦿ *Zhi Fang Wai Ji*, sample page

When interacting with Fujian literati and officialdom, Aleni paid particular attention to befriending the influential intelligentsia and officialdom from all over Fujian, who were the social foundation and backing of his missionary activities in Fujian. Many of them also gifted him poems that sing his praises. These poems are compiled in an anthology called *Min Zhong Zhu Gong Zeng Shi* (*Gift Poems from the Literati and Officials of Fujian*), which is believed to be a true portrayal of the missionary activities of the Jesuits in Fujian.

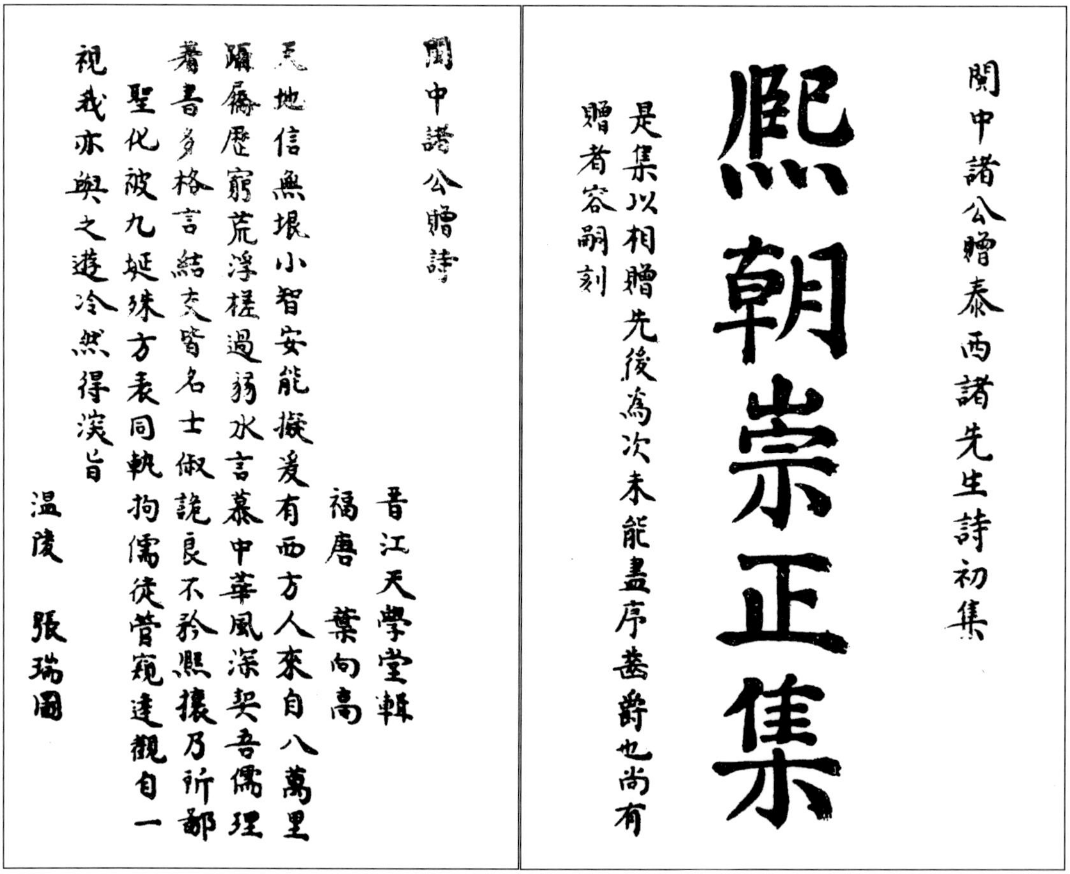

閩中諸公贈泰西諸先生詩初集

熙朝崇正集

是集以相贈先後為次未能盡序齒爵也尚有贈者容嗣刻

閩中諸公贈詩

晋江天學堂輯

福唐 葉向高

天地信無垠小智安能擬爰有西方人來自八萬里躡蹻歷窮荒浮槎過弱水言慕中華風深契吾儒理著書多格言結交皆名士俶詭良不矜熙攘乃所鄙聖化被九埏殊方表同軌拘儒徒管窺達觀自一視我亦與之遊泠然得深旨

温陵 張瑞圖

⦿ *Min Zhong Zhu Gong Zeng Shi* (*Xi Chao Chong Zheng Ji*), sample page

During the spread of Catholicism in Fujian during the Ming and Qing dynasties, the iconic event of the collision and mix of Chinese and Western cultures is undoubtedly *A Dialogue on God as the Creator and Governor of the Universe* (*San Shan Lun Xue*). It was a discussion between Fujian literati and officialdom, including Ye Xianggao and Cao Xuequan in the late Ming Dynasty and Aleni, on Catholicism and cultural differences between the East and the West. It reflects the interest, doubts, and curiosity that Western science triggered among the literati and officialdom in Fujian in the late Ming Dynasty and the questions about how Western science and Chinese ideology and culture should be adjusted when Chinese intellectuals absorbed Western science. The Jesuits gave them convincing answers, which became the ideological elements the Chinese literati and officialdom could understand and accept.

A Dialogue on God as the Creator and Governor of the Universe lasted for two days. In this ideological dialogue, the protagonists of both China and the West presented their ideological focus and cultural subconsciousness. Still, it opened up a deep discussion between the eastern and western ideological circles regarding life philosophies and spiritual beliefs at that time. It meant a great deal to the times.

⦿ Where *San Shan Lun Xue* happened: Furong Garden (present scene)

Sanshan Church, the first Catholic church in Fuzhou, was built by Aleni and Ye Xianggao's eldest grandson, Ye Yifan, during the reign of Ming Emperor Chongzhen (1628–1644). It is not only the first Catholic church in the history of Fuzhou but also the first built by Aleni since his missionary activity in Fujian.

The Jesuits who spread Catholicism in Fujian were supported and protected by Emperor Longwu of the Southern Ming regime. The Jesuits entrusted the development of Catholicism in Fujian to Emperor Longwu. However, the Longwu regime collapsed within two years, and so did the hopes of the Jesuits.

The turmoil in the late Ming and early Qing dynasties forced Aleni to spend his last few years in Fujian to avoid the war. With the fall of the Longwu regime and the demise of the Southern Ming Dynasty, Aleni's legendary life came to an end in 1649.

The tomb of Aleni

2 A Prairie Fire: The Chinese Rites Controversy in Fujian

The Chinese rites controversy between Chinese and Western Roman Catholic missionaries was a significant debate during the 17th and 18th centuries on the rituals of ancestor worship and Confucian worship in China. It took place in Fujian and reached a climax in Fujian, too. At last, Fujian literati and officialdom proposed to ban Catholicism, thus ending this controversy.

At the end of the Ming Dynasty, after the Jesuit Aleni came to Fujian, following Matteo Ricci's "adaptation" strategy, Catholic believers were allowed to worship ancestors and Confucius. Still, the religious orders within the Catholic Church (the Dominicans and the Franciscans) had different opinions on this. In 1632, the Dominican P. Juan Bautista de Morales and the Franciscan P. Antonio Caballero de Santa Maria came to study Chinese in Fu'an. When learning the word "worship," Caballero learned from the teacher that Chinese believers at that time could worship ancestors and Confucius. To find out the truth of this matter, Bautista and Caballero attended an ancestor worship ceremony held by Chinese believers at the Miao family ancestral hall in Muyang, Fu'an, and concluded that these rituals were superstitious and should be banned. Later, the two wrote a letter to Aleni, but he replied that the Chinese believers should be allowed to worship their ancestors, which annoyed Caballero terribly.

⦿ Dominican emblem on the tombstone

Catholic (Dominican) Cemetery

The Ancestral Hall of the Miao Family in Muyang, Fu'an

⦿ Catholic Church in in Muyang, Fu'an

In 1635, Bautista and Caballero came to Fuzhou. They had a meeting with Francois Furtado, the vice-president of the Jesuit Society at that time, to discuss the issue of ancestor worship for Chinese believers. The Jesuits held on to their original opinion. After the two sides negotiated to no avail, the friars began to collect evidence. In June 1637, Caballero personally sent evidence of Chinese believers worshipping their ancestors to Manila and requested the Archbishop of Manila to convene a conference, which theologians and religious jurists attended. Still, the Philippine Jesuits opposed it.

Later, the Archbishop of Manila wrote to the Pope, demanding to condemn the action of these Jesuits. The Jesuit Far East Inspector, Emmanuel Diaz Senior, immediately sent a letter to the Archbishop of Manila after obtaining a copy of the Pope's letter, refuting the friars' accusations one by one.

In 1643, Caballero personally traveled to Rome to lobby. In 1645, Pope Innocent X issued an encyclical prohibiting Chinese believers from participating in Confucian and ancestor worship ceremonies. In this way, the spark of the Chinese rites controversy was ignited by the interpretation of the word "worship." The flame burned from Fujian to Manila to Rome, and a prairie fire broke out throughout the East and the West. This incident eventually led to Emperor Kangxi's decision to ban the spread of Catholicism in China.

⊙ Catholic Church in Lankou, Ningde

⊙ Portrait of Pope Innocent X

⊙ Portrait of Emperor Kangxi

In the liturgical dispute, the literati and officialdom from Fujian who received Catholic teaching stood in support of the "adaptation" strategy of the Jesuits. They defended ancestor worship and Confucian worship in China. They argued that Chinese ancestor worship was not religious idol worship but only an act of reverence and remembrance for the ancestors. The representative writings related to this matter include *Li Su Ming Bian* by Li Liangjue, the son of Li Jiugong, a missionary in the Qing Dynasty, and *Li Shi Tiao Wen* (*On Worship, and Studies on Ancestral Worship*) by Yan Mo, a missionary/official in Zhangzhou.

The controversy over Chinese rites not only stirred an uproar in Fujian and Chinese society but also aroused widespread concern and discussion in Western European society. Because this controversy involved many aspects of Chinese Confucian culture, it also enabled Chinese ideology and culture to spread widely in European intellectual circles so that they could use relevant elements in Chinese culture to criticize Western European feudal autocracy and ideological imprisonment and started the Enlightenment movement.

3 The Westward Spread of Neo-Confucianism—The Spread and Influence of Cheng-Zhu School in the West

The Cheng-zhu School is the concentrated expression of Fujian's excellent traditional culture. Its spread and influence in the West is the most concrete evidence of the spread and influence of Fujian culture to the outside world. During the Ming and Qing dynasties, Cheng-zhu School was mainly transmitted to the West in three ways, and it had a broad and far-reaching impact on the West.

Because of the denial and criticism from Matteo Ricci and other Jesuits, the Cheng-zhu School was passively and unconsciously spread to the West. The stronger their opposition to the Cheng-zhu School, the more profound the influence of Neo-Confucianism in the West. And Matteo Ricci's *The True Meaning of the Lord of Heaven* is one of the most influential works of unintentional dissemination of Neo-Confucianism.

⦿ Portrait of Matteo Ricci

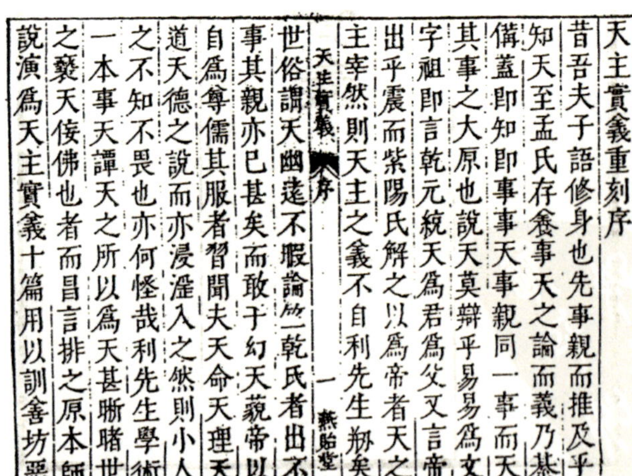

天主實義重刻序
昔吾夫子語修身也先事親而推及乎
知天至孟氏存養事天之論而義乃綦
備蓋即知即事事天事親同一事而天
其事之大原也說天莫辯乎易易爲文
字祖即言乾元統天爲君爲父又言帝
出乎震而紫陽氏解之以爲帝者天之
主宰然則天主之義不自利先生剏矣
天主實義 序 一 燕貽堂
世俗謂天幽遠不暇論竺乾氏者出不
事其親亦已甚矣而敢于幻天藐帝以
自爲尊儒其服者習聞夫天命天理天
道天德之說而亦浸淫入之然則小人
之不知不畏也亦何怪哉利先生學術
一本事天譚天之所以爲天甚晰睹世
之褻天佞佛也者而昌言排之原本師
說演爲天主實義十篇用以訓善坊惡

⦿ *The True Meaning of the Lord of Heaven*, sample page

Through the Jesuit symbolists' embrace of the Cheng-zhu School, Neo-Confucianism was positively and directly brought to the West. Symbolists not only fully accepted ancient Confucianism but also fully affirmed the Neo-Confucianism of the Song and Ming dynasties. Joseph de Prémare wrote letters entitled *Letters on Chinese Monotheism*, which gave a detailed introduction to the Cheng-zhu School.

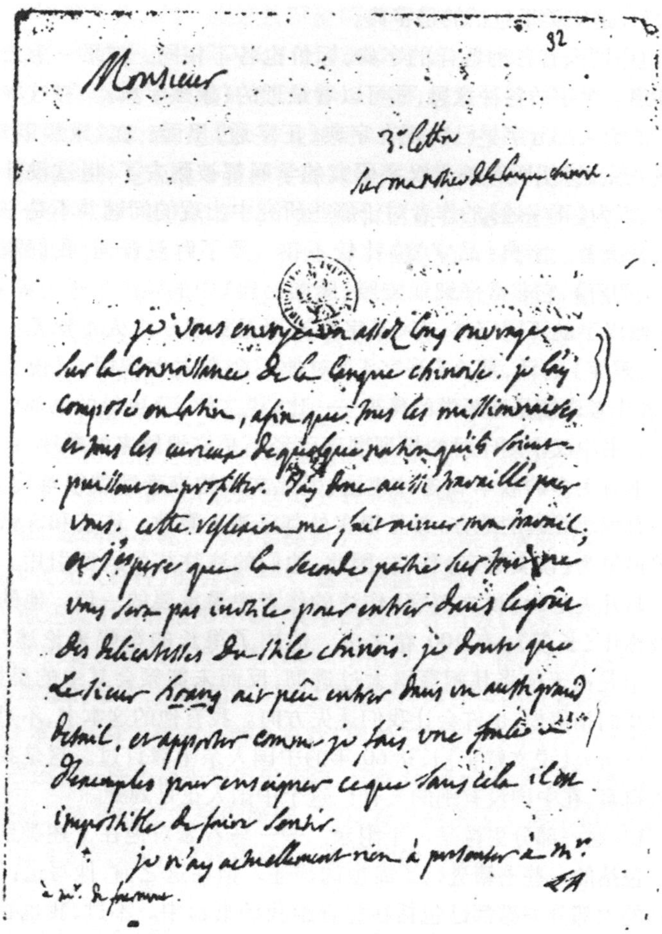

⦿ Manuscript of Joseph de Prémare's 1728 *Letters on Chinese Monotheism*

The Four Books, as translated by the Jesuits, unconsciously and indirectly spread the Cheng-zhu School to the West. *Notes on the Four Books* by Zhu Xi is one of his essential works of Confucianism. To teach Westerners more about Confucianism, since the end of the 1680s, the Jesuits continued to translate *The Four Books* into Western languages.

⦿ (LEFT) Portrait of Zhu Xi

⦿ (BELOW) *Notes on the Four Books*, sample page

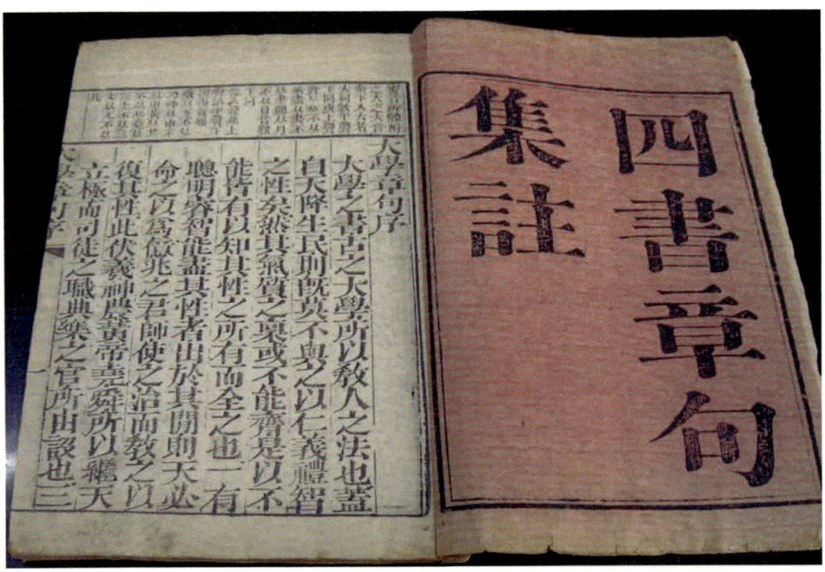

The Cheng-zhu School, which spread to the West during the Ming and Qing Dynasties, impacted thinkers and philosophers in different eras and camps in the West.

(1) **Influence on Western skepticism.**
In the 17th and 18th centuries, Western skepticism was the ideological weapon that progressive thinkers and philosophers wielded to attack and oppose the church and scholasticism. Its prominent representatives were Descartes and Peir.

(2) **Influence on occasionalism.**
The occasionalism has changed from Descartes' duality to the complete unity of religious idealism. Its primary representative is Malebranche, whose philosophical masterpiece is *Dialogue between a Christian Philosopher and a Chinese Philosopher on the Existence and Nature of God.*

(3) **Influence on French Enlightenment.**
Voltaire, the leader of the Enlightenment among the French bourgeoisie, was also influenced by the Cheng-zhu School.

(4) **Influence on Leibniz's Monadology.**
Monadology is the core of Leibniz's objective idealism system, and its connotation has many similarities with the Cheng-zhu School.

⦿ Portrait of Descartes

⦿ Portrait of Voltaire

⦿ Portrait of Leibniz

4 The Legendary Fujianese—The Earliest Fujianese Who Went to Europe during the Ming and Qing Dynasties

When Western missionaries preached in Fujian to cultivate Chinese clergy, they also sent young believers to study abroad. When they completed their studies, they returned to China, served as clergymen, and engaged in evangelistic work. These Fujianese, the first to go to Europe and devote themselves to the church, also actively introduced and spread traditional Chinese culture to the West and bridged the cultural exchanges between the East and the West.

The Dominican Order sent Luo Wenzao, a Catholic from Fu'an, to the Philippines to study the two subjects of Catholic doctrine and ethics. Later, Luo became the first Chinese bishop.

⦿ Portrait of Luo Wenzao

Huang Jialue, a native of Putian, Fujian, was born in a Catholic family. He went to Paris with Father Artus de Lionne. Soon, Huang was sent to Rome, where he continued his studies, and after being ordained a priest, he returned to China to preach.

⦿ Portrait of Huang Jialue

⦿ Portrait of Liang Hongren

⦿ *Huang Jialue and Early French Sinology*, cover

Huang Jialue was the first Chinese student to settle in Paris, and Montesquieu had multiple conversations with him. With the assistance of Huang Jialue, Montesquieu published *Persian Letters* and *The Spirit of the Law.*

After Huang Jialue settled in Paris, he devoted himself to the cultural exchange between China and France, which played a specific role in spreading Chinese thought and culture to France. Huang organized and translated Chinese books sent by missionaries to the French Royal Library. To a certain extent, it gave France an obvious advantage over other European countries in learning Chinese studies in the 19th century.

After Huang Jialue, five other Fujian students went to Europe during the reign of Emperor Qianlong of the Qing Dynasty (1736–1796). They were Cai Wen'an, Yan Yagu, Cai Ruoxiang, Yan Kuanren, and Yan Ganlin. All came from Longhai, Zhangzhou, and Fujian. They studied at Complesso del Cinesi in Italy and became clergymen after graduation.

⦿ Portrait of Montesquieu

⦿ *The Spirit of the Law*, Chinese translation, two volume edition

⦿ Hokkien students from Complesso dei Cinesi

CHAPTER 5

The World Tea Port—The Evolution of the Trade Patterns between Fujian and the West after the Opium War

After the Opium War, China opened up. Since Fujian was forced to open its trading ports, the scale and depth of trade between the East and the West reached a new level, and Fuzhou Port grew into a famous world tea port. Indeed, not all trade between China and the West was a fair exchange of goods. There was suffering and humiliation that came with the unequal treaties and the devastating opium trade and coolie trade.

1 From the "Queen of Black Tea" to the Adventure of Tea Mountain—Westerners' Pursuit and Investigation of Wuyi Black Tea

In 1662, Princess Catherine, the Queen of Black Tea from Portugal, brought Wuyi black tea into the British royal family as a dowry. Soon, a trend of Chinese tea drinking was set off in British and Western society, especially in Wuyi black tea and tea sets.

⦿ The Queen of Black Tea—Portrait of Princess Catherine

It was not until the end of the 18th century that black tea gained popularity in the lower classes, thus realizing its total popularization in British society. Drinking black tea changed British dining and lifestyle, becoming an indispensable part of the British diet.

⦿ Advertisement for the United Kingdom Tea Company

⊙ The painting of a European family drinking tea

The development of black tea has promoted the development of the British porcelain manufacturing industry. In the early 18th century, due to the limitation of raw materials and craftsmanship, the U.K. was relatively backward in manufacturing and mainly relied on importing Chinese porcelain. By the middle of the 18th century, great progress had been made in the British porcelain manufacturing industry, and the trial production of the famous milky white porcelain and jasper porcelain successively succeeded.

⊙ A tea set for drinking black tea

To obtain information about Chinese tea, Westerners traveled across the sea to Fujian and went deep into the inland areas of Fujian to investigate the local tea of Fujian.

From 1831 to 1833, German missionary Charles Gutzlaff inspected the coast of China. From November 1834 to May 1835, Gutzlaff, together with G. J. Gordon, a British opium dealer, and E. Stevens, an American missionary, made two illegal expeditions by boat into the Min River, where they collected intelligence on tea cultivation in the mountains around the river.

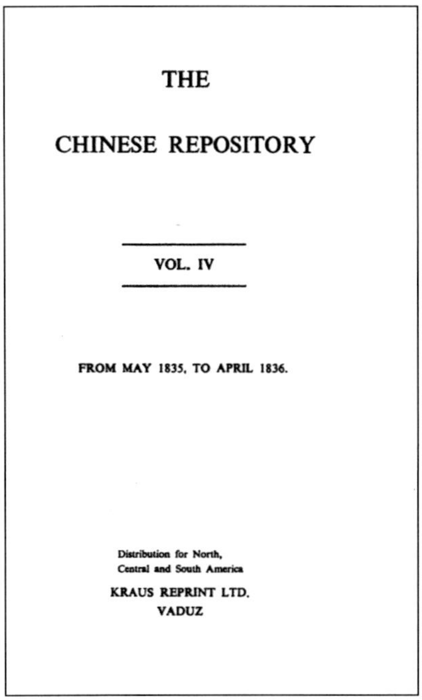

THE

CHINESE REPOSITORY

VOL. IV

FROM MAY 1835, TO APRIL 1836.

Distribution for North, Central and South America

KRAUS REPRINT LTD.
VADUZ

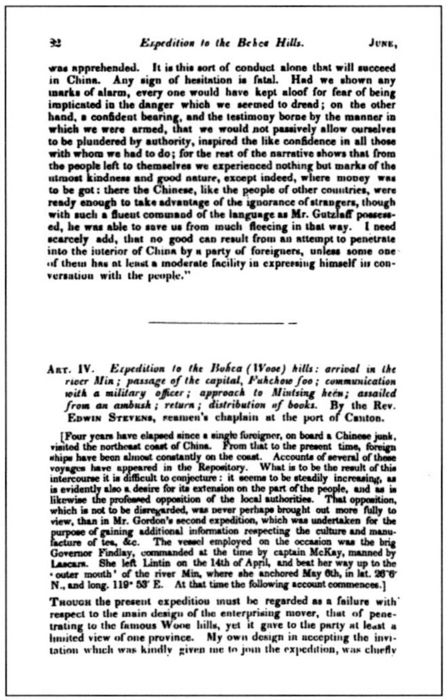

32 *Expedition to the Bohea Hills.* JUNE,

was apprehended. It is this sort of conduct alone that will succeed in China. Any sign of hesitation is fatal. Had we shown any marks of alarm, every one would have kept aloof for fear of being implicated in the danger which we seemed to dread; on the other hand, a confident bearing, and the testimony borne by the manner in which we were armed, that we would not passively allow ourselves to be plundered by authority, inspired the like confidence in all those with whom we had to do; for the rest of the narrative shows that from the people left to themselves we experienced nothing but marks of the utmost kindness and good nature, except indeed, where money was to be got: there the Chinese, like the people of other countries, were ready enough to take advantage of the ignorance of strangers, though with such a fluent command of the language as Mr. Gutzlaff possessed, he was able to save us from much fleecing in that way. I need scarcely add, that no good can result from an attempt to penetrate into the interior of China by a party of foreigners, unless some one of them has at least a moderate facility in expressing himself in conversation with the people."

ART. IV. *Expedition to the Bohea (Wooe) hills: arrival in the river Min; passage of the capital, Fuhchow foo; communication with a military officer; approach to Mintsing heën; assailed from an ambush; return; distribution of books.* By the Rev. EDWIN STEVENS, seamen's chaplain at the port of Canton.

[Four years have elapsed since a single foreigner, on board a Chinese junk, visited the northeast coast of China. From that to the present time, foreign ships have been almost constantly on the coast. Accounts of several of these voyages have appeared in the Repository. What is to be the result of this intercourse it is difficult to conjecture: it seems to be steadily increasing, as is evidently also a desire for its extension on the part of the people, and as is likewise the professed opposition of the local authorities. That opposition, which is not to be disregarded, was never perhaps brought out more fully to view, than in Mr. Gordon's second expedition, which was undertaken for the purpose of gaining additional information respecting the culture and manufacture of tea, &c. The vessel employed on the occasion was the brig Governor Findlay, commanded at the time by captain McKay, manned by Lascars. She left Lintin on the 14th of April, and beat her way up to the 'outer mouth' of the river Min, where she anchored May 6th, in lat. 26°6' N., and long. 119° 53' E. At that time the following account commences.]

THOUGH the present expedition must be regarded as a failure with respect to the main design of the enterprising mover, that of penetrating to the famous Wooe hills, yet it gave to the party at least a limited view of one province. My own design in accepting the invitation which was kindly given me to join the expedition, was chiefly

⦿ Records of the adventure in tea mountains in *The Chinese Repository*

Robert Fortune, a notorious tea thief, was dispatched by the British East India Company in the middle of the 19th century to travel deep into the Chinese tea villages. He contrived to take Chinese tea-growing and tea-making techniques back to the West, thus changing the market structure of the tea trade between China and the West. This dealt a devasting blow to China's tea sales, and its trade surplus became a deficit. Economists believe he did more harm to the Chinese economy than an entire army and call him the deadliest commercial spy in history.

⦿ Portrait of Robert Fortune

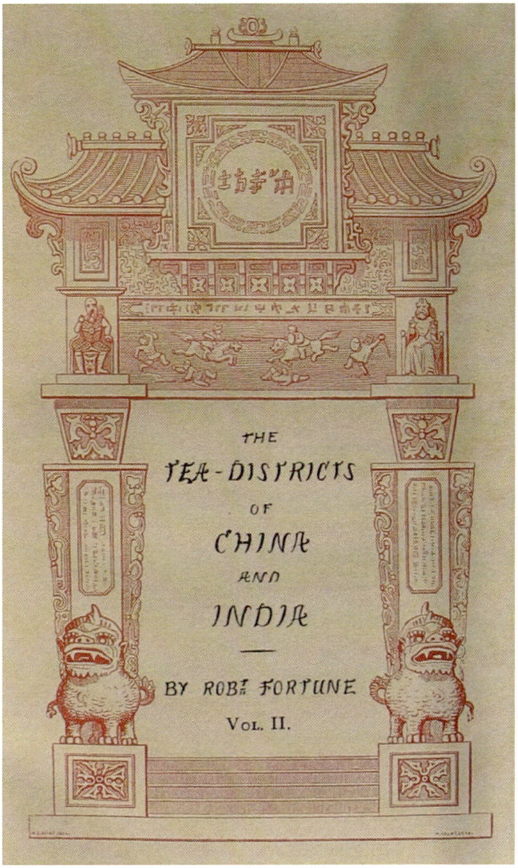

⦿ *The Tea Districts of China and India, Volume 2,* by Robert Fortune, cover

2 After the Opening of the Port—The In-Depth Development of the Fuzhou Tea Market and Sino-Western Trade

The Treaty of Nanjing between China and the U.K. expressly stipulated that Fuzhou be opened as a trading port city. Its ultimate goal was to enable direct trade between the U.K. and local Fujianese tea merchants.

⊙ The prosperity of trade in Fuzhou Port after it was opened

With the opening of trade in Fuzhou in the late Qing Dynasty, foreign business people and missionaries poured into Fuzhou in large numbers. Various countries established consulates in Fuzhou to handle exchange affairs with China.

⊙ The former site of the British Consulate in Fuzhou

⊙ The former site of the Dutch Consulate in Fuzhou

⊙ The former site of the U.S. Consulate in Fuzhou

⊙ The former site of the Russian Consulate in Fuzhou

Because of the in-depth interaction of trade between China and foreign countries, tremendous market demand boosted the development of Fuzhou's local economy, especially the tea trade, which presented a new look. From 1853 to the mid-1880s, the export volume of tea from Fuzhou had always been on the rise, making Fuzhou one of the three major tea ports in China at the time. American missionary Justin Doolittle described the busy Fuzhou tea market and the prosperity of the tea trade in the middle of the 19th century in his book *A Vocabulary and Hand-book of the Chinese Language.*

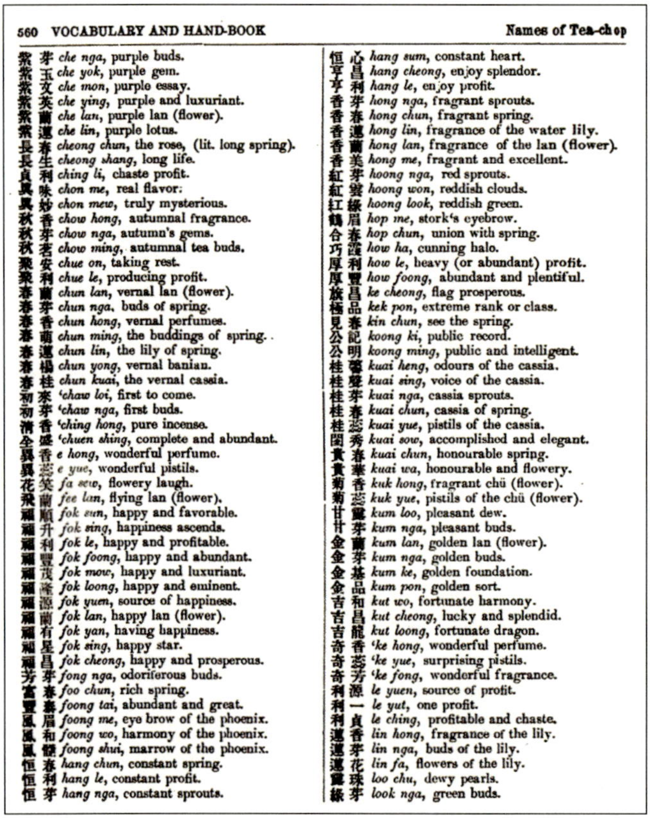

560 VOCABULARY AND HAND-BOOK | Names of Tea-chop

紫芽 *che nga*, purple buds.
紫玉 *che yok*, purple gem.
紫文 *che mon*, purple essay.
紫英 *che ying*, purple and luxuriant.
紫蘭 *che lan*, purple lan (flower).
紫蓮 *che lin*, purple lotus.
長春 *cheong chun*, the rose, (lit. long spring).
長生 *cheong shang*, long life.
貞利 *ching li*, chaste profit.
眞味 *chon me*, real flavor.
眞妙 *chon mew*, truly mysterious.
秋香 *chow hong*, autumnal fragrance.
秋芽 *chow nga*, autumn's gems.
秋茗 *chow ming*, autumnal tea buds.
聚安 *chue on*, taking rest.
聚利 *chue le*, producing profit.
春蘭 *chun lan*, vernal lan (flower).
春芽 *chun nga*, buds of spring.
春香 *chun hong*, vernal perfumes.
春萌 *chun ming*, the buddings of spring.
春蓮 *chun lin*, the lily of spring.
春榕 *chun yong*, vernal banian.
春桂 *chun kuai*, the vernal cassia.
初來 *'chaw loi*, first to come.
初芽 *'chaw nga*, first buds.
清香 *'ching hong*, pure incense.
全盛 *'chuen shing*, complete and abundant.
異香 *e hong*, wonderful perfume.
異蕊 *e yue*, wonderful pistils.
花笑 *fa sew*, flowery laugh.
飛蘭 *fee lan*, flying lan (flower).
福順 *fok sun*, happy and favorable.
福升 *fok sing*, happiness ascends.
福利 *fok le*, happy and profitable.
福豐 *fok foong*, happy and abundant.
福茂 *fok mow*, happy and luxuriant.
福隆 *fok loong*, happy and eminent.
福源 *fok yuen*, source of happiness.
福蘭 *fok lan*, happy lan (flower).
福有 *fok yan*, having happiness.
福星 *fok sing*, happy star.
福昌 *fok cheong*, happy and prosperous.
芳芽 *fong nga*, odoriferous buds.
富春 *foo chun*, rich spring.
豐泰 *foong tai*, abundant and great.
鳳眉 *foong me*, eye brow of the phoenix.
鳳和 *foong wo*, harmony of the phoenix.
鳳髓 *foong shui*, marrow of the phoenix.
恒春 *hang chun*, constant spring.
恒利 *hang le*, constant profit.
恒芽 *hang nga*, constant sprouts.
恒心 *hang sum*, constant heart.
亨昌 *hang cheong*, enjoy splendor.
亨利 *hang le*, enjoy profit.
香芽 *hong nga*, fragrant sprouts.
香春 *hong chun*, fragrant spring.
香蓮 *hong lin*, fragrance of the water lily.
香蘭 *hong lan*, fragrance of the lan (flower).
香美 *hong me*, fragrant and excellent.
紅芽 *hoong nga*, red sprouts.
紅雲 *hoong won*, reddish clouds.
紅綠 *hoong look*, reddish green.
鶴眉 *hop me*, stork's eyebrow.
合春 *hop chun*, union with spring.
巧霞 *how ha*, cunning halo.
厚利 *how le*, heavy (or abundant) profit.
厚豐 *how foong*, abundant and plentiful.
旗昌 *ke cheong*, flag prosperous.
極品 *kek pon*, extreme rank or class.
見春 *kin chun*, see the spring.
公記 *koong ki*, public record.
公明 *koong ming*, public and intelligent.
桂馨 *kuai heng*, odours of the cassia.
桂聲 *kuai sing*, voice of the cassia.
桂芽 *kuai nga*, cassia sprouts.
桂春 *kuai chun*, cassia of spring.
桂蕊 *kuai yue*, pistils of the cassia.
閨秀 *kuai sow*, accomplished and elegant.
貴春 *kuai chun*, honourable spring.
貴華 *kuai wa*, honourable and flowery.
菊香 *kuk hong*, fragrant chü (flower).
菊蕊 *kuk yue*, pistils of the chü (flower).
甘露 *kum loo*, pleasant dew.
甘芽 *kum nga*, pleasant buds.
金蘭 *kum lan*, golden lan (flower).
金芽 *kum nga*, golden buds.
金基 *kum ke*, golden foundation.
金品 *kum pon*, golden sort.
吉和 *kut wo*, fortunate harmony.
吉昌 *kut cheong*, lucky and splendid.
吉龍 *kut loong*, fortunate dragon.
奇香 *'ke hong*, wonderful perfume.
奇蕊 *'ke yue*, surprising pistils.
奇芳 *'ke fong*, wonderful fragrance.
利源 *le yuen*, source of profit.
利一 *le yut*, one profit.
利貞 *le ching*, profitable and chaste.
蓮香 *lin hong*, fragrance of the lily.
蓮芽 *lin nga*, buds of the lily.
蓮花 *lin fa*, flowers of the lily.
露珠 *loo chu*, dewy pearls.
綠芽 *look nga*, green buds.

⦿ *A Vocabulary and Hand-book of the Chinese Language,* sample page

⦿ Portrait of Justin Doolittle

The tea market's prosperity has propelled the urban economy's development. After the opening of the Fuzhou port in the late Qing Dynasty, the number of foreign companies and foreign businessmen who came to Fuzhou to engage in commercial trade continued to increase. Export black tea was classified and packaged in Fuzhou before being shipped to the West. This promoted the rise of the barge transportation industry in the Min River in the late Qing Dynasty because the watercourse of the Min River was too narrow for large ships to pass, and small ships were required to load the goods of large ships and transport them to large ships anchored in Mawei. This was also true for the shipment of foreign goods to Fuzhou City.

⦿ The former site of the American Chinese Company

⦿ The former site of Dodwell & Co., Ltd.

⦿ The former site of Chun Kee Tea Shop

⦿ Commercial Street in Nantai, Fuzhou

⦿ Cargo barge of the Dan people of Min River

⦿ Russell & Co. (1870s)

⦿ The economic prosperity area of the estuary of the Min River in Nantai

The rise of the tea market changed the original social condition of Fuzhou, and some new occupations appeared, such as tea tasters and professional brokers specializing in the tea trade. There were also tea shops with modern business models on the streets of Fuzhou, leaving the imprint of the early changes of Chinese tea shops that had absorbed Western business modes.

Because of the prosperity of the tea trade, the clipper ships that trafficked tea to the West also set off a wave of tea transportation competitions. The starting point of the tea transportation competition was the Luoxing Pagoda in Fuzhou Port, and the finish lines were the Royal Docks in the U.K., the New York Port in New England in the U.S., and the Port of Providence, Rhode Island. In December 1868, Western artist James Henry Butt painted a watercolor painting entitled *Luoxing Pagoda, Fuzhou*, which depicts the scene of a clipper ship transporting Fujian tea.

⊙ A tea shop in Fuzhou in the late Qing Dynasty

A clipper ship

Port of Providence, Rhode Island

⊙ *Luoxing Pagoda*, a watercolor by James Henry Butt

⊙ Royal Docks of the U.K. in the Industrial Revolution

Fujian tea was not only an important commodity in global trade but also the fuse of major historical events worldwide. The tea in the Boston Tea Party that kicked off the American Revolutionary War was Wuyi tea. Once the U.S. declared independence in 1776, the merchant ship *Empress of China* was dispatched to transport tea from China to the U.S. for the first time in 1785 and made huge profits. After that, it started a wave of American businessmen's tea trade in China, especially importing tea from Fujian.

⦿ 19th century New York Port

⦿ Boston Tea Party

3 The Coolie Trade—The Miserable Past of Chinese Laborers Abroad

The development of the modern capitalist economy has multiplied the demand for cheap overseas labor. Meanwhile, Fujian faced political oppression and economic plunder by foreign capitalism. During this period, the emigration of Fujianese workers overseas reached an unprecedented climax.

Statistics record that the Western colonists' plundering of Chinese workers started in Xiamen. Xiamen was one of the earliest trading port cities opened. Gulangyu was a public concession in modern Fujian. Western countries built consulates and affiliated buildings there. It was one of the centers of Westerners' activities on the southeast coast of China. In the middle of the 19th century, the coolie trade in Xiamen developed widely, and Xiamen Port became one of the main ports for the coolie trade and Chinese laborers to go abroad.

⦿ The coolies crowded densely on a ship

For the U.S., since the victory of the War of Independence, as reclamation and cultivation of land, mining, and railway construction required lots of labor, in 1868, the U.S. government and the Qing government signed the Burlingame Treaty, under the protection of which, the American capitalists blatantly plundered China's cheap labor force by all means.

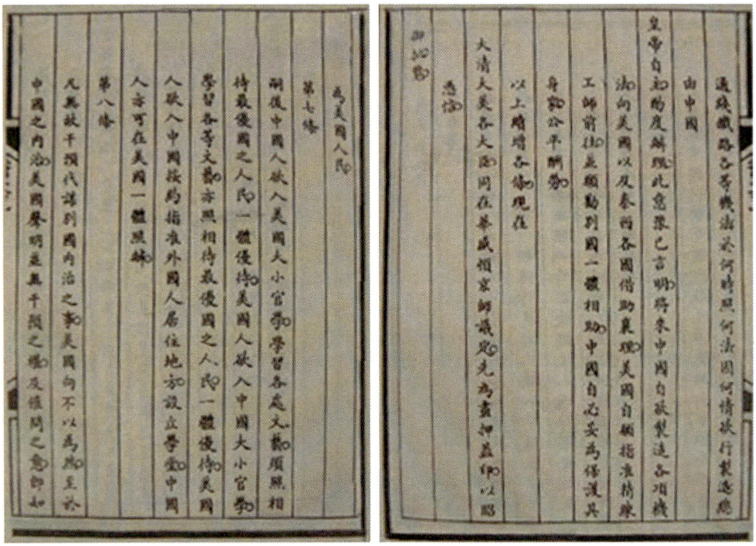

為美國人民

第七條

嗣後中國人欲入美國大小官學學習各處文藝須照相
待最優國之人民一體優待美國人欲入中國大小官學
學習各等文藝亦照相待最優國之人民一體優待美國
人欲入中國按約指准外國人居住地方設立學堂中國
人亦可在美國一體照辦

第八條

凡無故干預代謀別國內治之事美國向不以為然至於
中國之內治美國聲明並無干預之權及催問之意即如

通線鐵路各等機法於何時照何法因何情欲行製造總
由中國
皇帝自主酌度辦理此意業已言明將來中國自欲製造各項機
法向美國以及泰西各國借助襄理美國自願指准精練
工師前往並願勸別國一體相助中國自必妥為保護其
身家公平酬勞
以上增續各條現在
大清大美各大臣同在華盛頓京都議定先為畫押蓋印以昭
信守
御批

⦿ (LEFT) The Burlingame Treaty, sample page

⦿ (BELOW) The Burlingame Treaty, signing

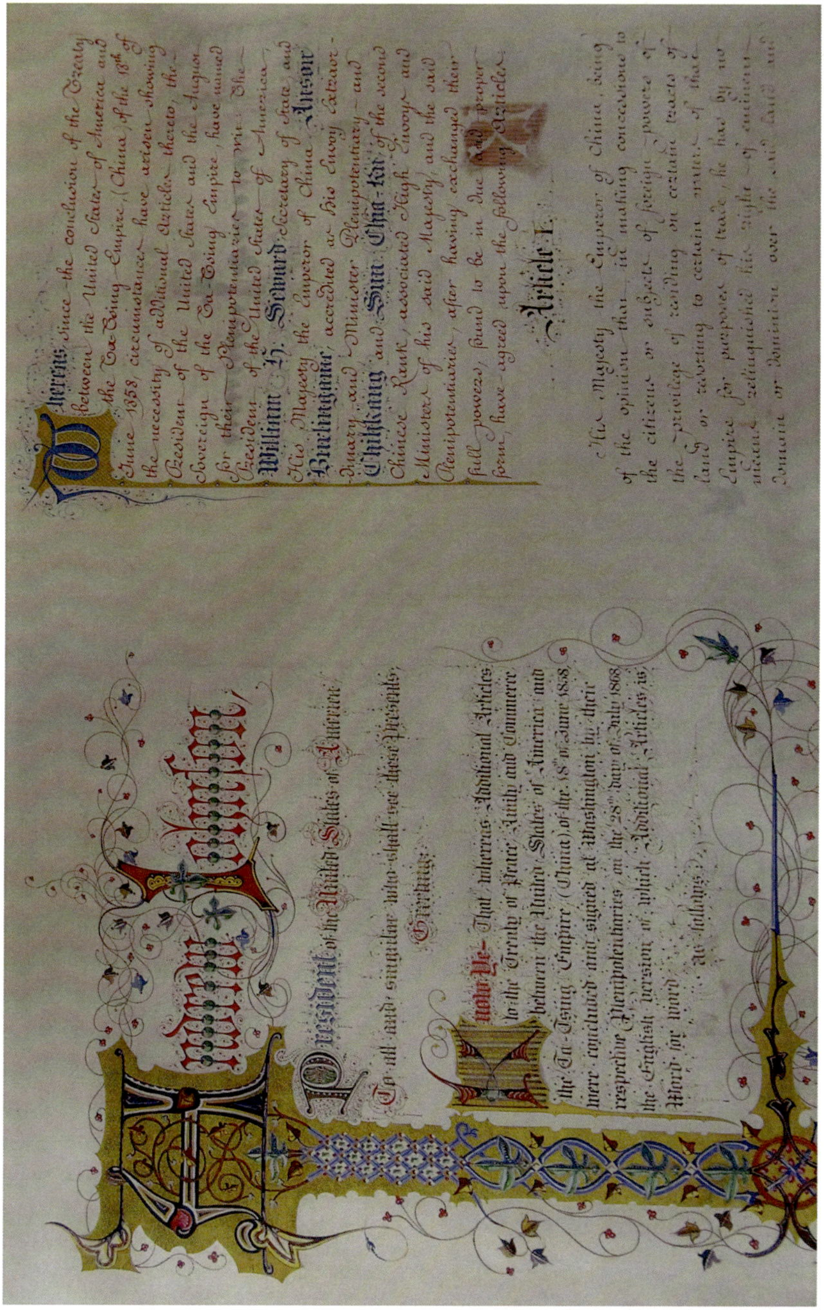

⊙ The Burlingame Treaty, English document

After emigrating to the Americas, Fujianese workers were brutally abused in forced labor. Still, they made outstanding contributions to local production and construction, such as railway construction, mining and gold panning, and farming. The book *History of Chinese Workers in Peru (1849–1874)* pointed out that during the entire period of imported immigrants, most of the labor produced was from the Chinese.

⦿ Chinese miners in the San Francisco gold rush

⦿ *History of Chinese Workers in Peru* (1849–1874), cover

In modern times, when Westerners came to recruit Chinese workers in Fujian, they usually had to sign an indenture. An original copy of the indenture of Chinese laborers in the Quanzhou City Archives depicts the situation before. This is a historical document of the people from Quanzhou, Fujian, who worked in America as indentured laborers during the reign of Emperor Xianfeng (1851–1861) in the Qing Dynasty.

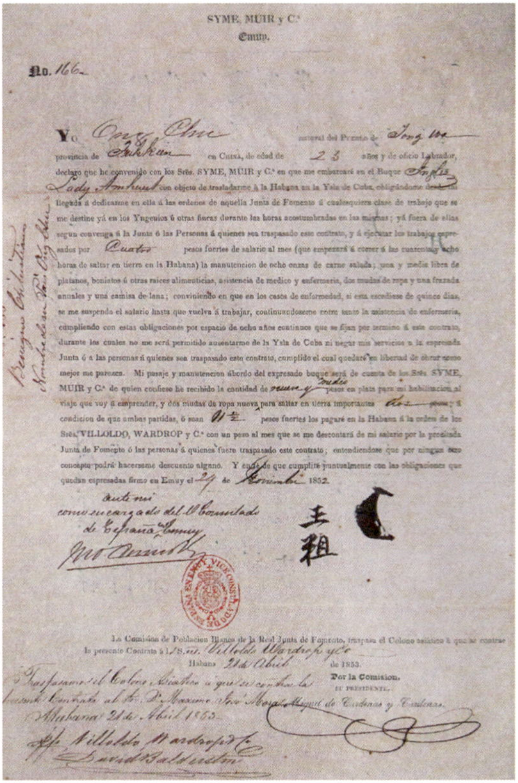

SYME, MUIR y Cª
Emuy.

No. 166

Yo Ong Chue natural del Pueblo de Tong Wa provincia de Fuhkien en China, de edad de 23 años y de oficio Labrador, declaro que he convenido con los Srês. SYME, MUIR y Cª en que me embarcaré en el Buque Ingles Lady Amherst con objeto de trasladarme á la Habana en la Ysla de Cuba, obligándome desde mi llegada á dedicarme en ella á las ordenes de aquella Junta de Fomento á cualesquiera clase de trabajo que se me destine yá en los Yngenios ó otras fincas durante las horas acostumbradas en las mismas; yá fuera de ellas segun convenga á la Junta ó las Personas á quienes sea traspasado este contrato, y á ejecutar los trabajos espresados por Cuatro pesos fuertes de salario al mes (que empezará á correr á las cuarenta y ocho horas de saltar en tierra en la Habana) la manutencion de ocho onzas de carne salada, una y media libra de platanos, boniatos ó otras raices alimenticias, asistencia de medico y enfermeria, dos mudas de ropa y una frazada annales y una camisa de lana; conviniendo en que en los casos de enfermedad, si esta escediese de quince dias, se me suspenda el salario hasta que vuelva á trabajar, continuandoseme entre tanto la asistencia de enfermeria, cumpliendo con estas obligaciones por espacio de ocho años continuos que se fijan por termino á este contrato, durante los cuales no me será permitido ausentarme de la Ysla de Cuba ni negar mis servicios a la espresada Junta ó a las personas á quienes sea traspasado este contrato, cumplido el cual quedaré en libertad de obrar como mejor me parezca. Mi pasaje y manutencion ábordo del espresado buque será de cuenta de los Srês. SYME, MUIR y Cª de quien confieso he recibido la cantidad de nueve y medio pesos en plata para mi habilitacion al viaje que voy á emprender, y dos mudas de ropa nueva para saltar en tierra importantes dos pesos; á condicion de que ambas partidas, ó sean 11½ pesos fuertes los pagaré en la Habana á la orden de los Srês. VILLOLDO, WARDROP y Cª con un peso al mes que se me descontará de mi salario por la precitada Junta de Fomento ó las personas á quienes fuere traspasado este contrato; entendiendose que por ningun otro concepto podrá hacerseme descuento alguno. Y en fé de que cumpliré puntualmente con las obligaciones que quedan espresadas firmo en Emuy el 29 de Noviembre 1852.

ante mi
como encargado del Vice Consulado
de España en Emuy

王粗

La Comision de Poblacion Blanca de la Real Junta de Fomento, traspasa el Colono asiatico á que se contrae la presente Contrata á los Srs. Villoldo Wardrop y Co.
Habana 21 de Abril de 1853.
Por la Comision,
EL PRESIDENTE.

Habana 21 de Abril 1853

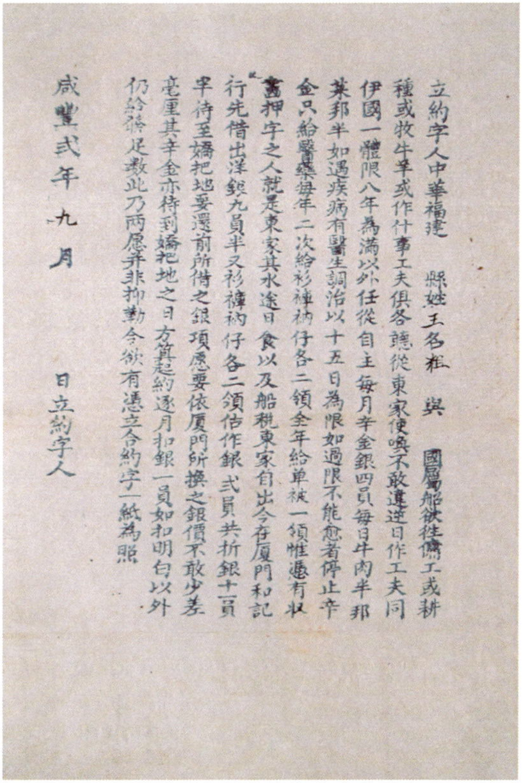

立約字人中華福建　縣姓王名粗　與　國屬船欲往傭工或耕
種或牧牛羊或作什事工夫俱各聽從東家使喚不敢違逆日作工夫同
伊國一體限八年為滿以外任從自主每月辛金銀四員每日牛肉半邦
菜邦半如遇疾病有醫生調治以十五日為限如過限不能愈者停止辛
金只給醫藥每年二次給衫褲衲仔各二領全年給单被一領惟憑有収
畫押字之人就是東家其水途日食以及船稅東家自出今在厦門和記
行先借出洋銀九員半又衫褲衲仔各二領估作銀弍員共折銀十一員
半待至嫡把地要還前所借之銀項愿要依厦門所換之銀價不敢少差
毫厘其辛金亦待到嫡把地之日方算起約逐月扣銀一員如扣明白以外
仍給辛足數此乃兩愿并非抑勒今欲有憑立合約字一紙為照

咸豐弍年九月　日立約字人

⦿ An indenture of Chinese laborers (front)

⦿ An indenture of Chinese laborers (back)

The Ryukyu Chinese cemetery is a Chinese cemetery located in Kannonzaki, Ishigaki City, Okinawa Prefecture, Japan, where over 100 Chinese laborers who died on the ship called *Robert Bowne* are buried.

⦿ Ryukyu Chinese cemetery

CHAPTER 6

Echoes between the East and the West—Deep Interactions between Modern Fujian and the Cultural Exchanges between China and the West

In the mid-19th century, China and the West's communications and cultural exchanges deepened. When preaching Christianity in Fujian, Christian missionaries came with many matters that represented the new civilization of the West, such as Western-style education, medical care, Western science and technology, and sports culture, which have had an important impact on the historical development of modern Fujian.

During this period, the best of Fujian culture was translated and spread to the West, setting off a climax of Fujian science going to the West. Meanwhile, excellent works of Western science, technology, culture, and ideology were translated and introduced to China, which enlightened the Chinese intellectuals.

1 Learn from the West—Fujian Pioneers

In modern Chinese history, Fujian was where cultural exchanges between China and the West took place. After the Opium War, people of insight in the Qing government began to realize the necessity of learning advanced military technology and science from the West. Senior officials in Fujian, represented by Lin Zexu and Xu Jiyu, compiled and published books that introduced various aspects of Western information with excellent foresight, leading the trend of the times.

⊙ Statue of Lin Zexu

Confronted with the pride and arrogance of the Western invaders, Lin Zexu was neither intimidated by their sharp weapons nor denied or despised their advanced technology. Instead, he was the first to propose learning Western skills. To understand Western countries' political, economic, and military situation for diplomacy at that time, he assembled a team to translate and collect materials from foreign newspapers and periodicals to compile the *Macau News Print*. He also organized the editing and translation of many foreign works on geography and technology, such as *Treatises on The Four Continents*. Lin Zexu deserves to be called the first person in modern China to advocate the learning of Western science and the opening of a path of learning. His motto "the ocean is vast for it admits all rivers" profoundly reflects his inclusiveness and openness. It has become one of the fundamental connotations of Fuzhou's city's humanistic spirit and "Fujian spirit."

⊙ A couplet of Lin Zexu's motto

During his tenure in Quanzhou and Xiamen, Xu Jiyu devoted himself to collecting foreign historical and geographical materials. *Ying Huan Zhi Lue* (*Brief Account of the Maritime Circuit*), compiled by him, was a book with the highest level of systematic introduction to world history and geography written by Chinese at that time. In the 1860s, it became a must-read for the Chinese to understand the general situation of the world. The translation of names of people, places, and countries in the book later became the standard for translating texts in foreign languages by Zongli Yamen (Office for the General Management of Affairs Concerning the Various Countries). In the late Qing Dynasty, Chinese of ideals and integrity who pursued new knowledge all absorbed ideas beneficial to the salvation of the Chinese nation from *Ying Huan Zhi Lue*.

⊙ Xu Jiyu

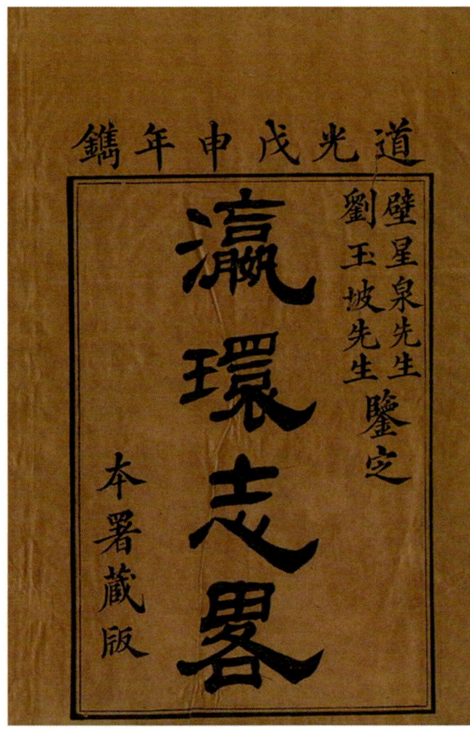

⊙ *Ying Huan Zhi Lue*, cover

In *Ying Huan Zhi Lue*, Xu Jiyu introduced not only the local customs and conditions around the world but also the Western democratic system for the first time and spoke highly of it.

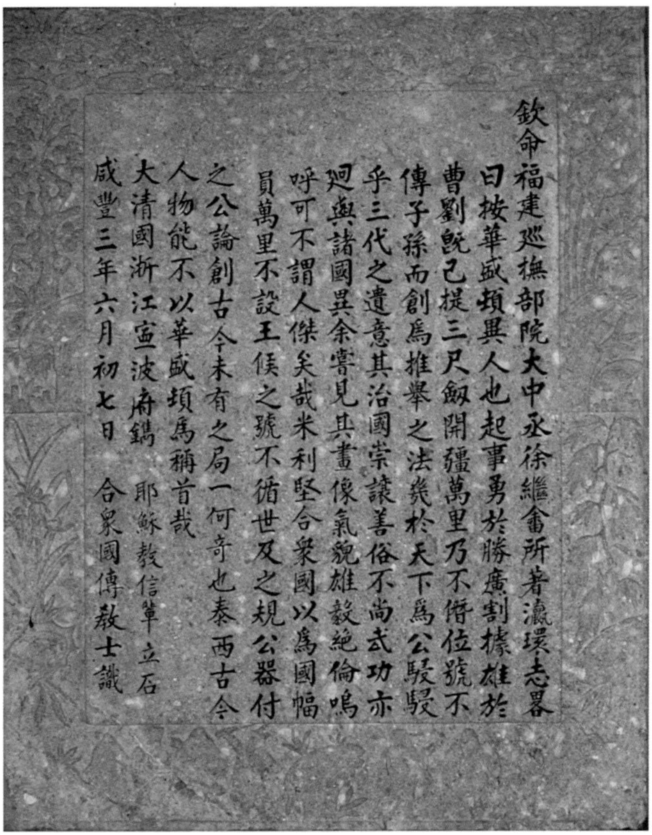

⦿ Chinese inscription in the Washington Monument

Ding Gongchen (1800–1875) was born in Jinjiang, Fujian in 1800. In 1831, Ding went abroad with foreign merchant ships to make a living. During his several years abroad, he paid particular attention to inspecting foreign ships, mainly European and American ships and guns, and studied Western weapons and machinery. Ding returned to China in 1840 when the Opium Wars broke out. Ambitious to serve his motherland, he actively improved

China's artillery and worked hard to compile and publish the military technology book *Yan Pao Tu Shu* (*Illustrated Artillery*), which gave a detailed account of the manufacture and application of various guns, gunpowder, ships and warships, and illustrations were attached. Based on absorbing the essence of ancient weapon books and referring to the theory of advanced weapons in the West, this book became a relatively advanced and complete weapon monograph in modern China and was applied in practice.

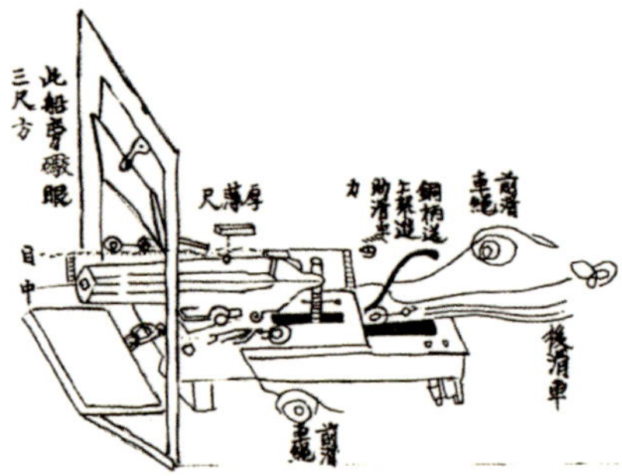

⦿ (LEFT) Painting of Ding Gongchen

⦿ (ABOVE) An illustration of *Illustrated Artillery*, American Carron cannons and their mounts

⦿ *Illustrated Artillery*, sample page

2 Look at the East and the West—Christian Missionaries in Fujian and Cultural Exchange between China and the West

The arrival of Christian missionaries in China is an important phenomenon in China's modern history, as they kicked off a new round of cultural exchanges between China and foreign countries. Missionaries had been in contact with Fujian since the 1830s and came to Fujian one after another after the Opium War. They were active there for over 100 years, building a new bridge of cultural exchange between China and the West.

On February 24, 1842, the first American missionaries to China—William Jones Boone from the Episcopal Church and David Abeel from the Reformed Church arrived on Gulangyu Island and set up a mission station on the island. In March 1842, they sailed to preach in Xiamen and distributed gospel booklets, which opened the prelude to the spread of modern Christianity in Fujian.

⊙ Portrait of William Jones Boone

John Van Nest Talmage, a reverend of the Reformed Church, preached in Xiamen for 42 years since he came to the city in 1847. He made significant contributions to the cultural exchanges between China and the West. In 1874, his eldest daughter Katherine Talmage and his second daughter Mary Elizabeth Talmage came to Xiamen, too. They were actively involved in women's evangelism and education.

⦿ Portrait of John Van Nest Talmage

⦿ John Van Nest Talmage, and his wife and daughters

⦿ Portrait of Katherine Talmage

⦿ Xiamen Xinjie Christian Church today

Xiamen Xinjie Christian Church was founded in 1848. As the first church founded by the Reformed Church in Fujian in modern times, it is known as the first sanctuary in China.

On January 2, 1847, Stephen Johnson, a missionary from the Congregational Church in the U.S., arrived in Rongcheng, kicking off the spread of modern Christianity in Fuzhou, and continuously modernizing Fuzhou's social undertakings.

Longtau Church was the first church founded in Fuzhou by the Methodist Episcopal Church in 1856. It is known as the first sanctuary in East Asia. Fuzhou was also the starting point for the Methodist Episcopal Church in Asia, which later radiated to Japan, the Korean Peninsula, and other places, with Fujian as the center.

Church of Heavenly Peace is another central church built by Methodist Episcopal Church in Fuzhou after Longtau Church. As the majority of Westerners moved to the Cangqian Mountain area in Fuzhou, it gradually developed into the headquarter of Methodist Episcopal Church in Fuzhou and radiated and extended from there to promote the missionary cause of the Methodist Episcopal Church in the province.

⦿ Longtau Church

⦿ Church of Heavenly Peace

St. John's Church was built in 1861 by British expatriates living in Fuzhou with the help of the British Consulate. After it was completed, not only British expatriates went there for mass, but also many Christians from other western countries chose to conduct religious activities there, hence its nickname, the "international church."

When Christianity spread in Fujian, it also opened up a Taiwanese diocese on the other side of the Taiwan Strait. James Laidlaw Maxwell was the first English Presbyterian missionary sent to Taiwan. He laid the foundation for the spread and development of Christianity in Taiwan.

The full name of Thai-Ping-Keng Church is Thai-Ping-Keng Maxwell Memorial Church. It is located next to the ring of Minsheng Green Park in Tainan. It commemorates Maxwell, who entered Taiwan and started preaching. It is one of the earliest Presbyterian churches in Taiwan.

⊙ St. John's Church

⦿ (LEFT) James Laidlaw Maxwell

⦿ (BELOW) Thai-Ping-Keng Church

In addition to Protestantism, the traditional Catholic forces were also active. They also radiated and extended outward from the two central bases of Fuzhou and Xiamen.

Saint Dominic's Cathedral, Fuzhou, located in Changpudun, Fanchuanpu, Cangshan District, Fuzhou City, is the largest Catholic church in Fujian Province. It was founded by the Spanish Dominican Order fin 1864. This magnificent cathedral is known as the number one cathedral south of the Yangtze River.

Xiamen Catholic Church sits at 15 Ci'an Road, Siming District, Xiamen, and was built in 1860. At first, it was the Xiamen Office of the Vicars of Fujian, and from 1883 to 1918, it was the cathedral of the Xiamen Diocese. In 1916, the bishop's residence was moved to Gulangyu Island, now the Gulangyu Catholic Church. The Xiamen Catholic Church became the office of the Dominican Order and the activity center of the Spanish Dominican missionaries.

⦿ (ABOVE) Saint Dominic's Cathedral, Fuzhou

⦿ (ABOVE RIGHT) Gulangyu Catholic Church

⦿ (RIGHT) Xiamen Catholic Church (St. Dominic's Church, Xiamen)

While modern Christianity was preached in Fujian, many new schools and academies were established, and modern Western courses and art were taught. Ying Wa College was an exemplary school for Christian secondary schools in Fujian. The Christian Church has also founded two higher education institutions in Fujian—Hwa Nan College and Fukien Christian University, demonstrating the vigorous development of new education in Fujian.

⦿ Wen Shan Girls' High School

⦿ Graduates of Wen Shan Girls' High School

⦿ Helin Tower, Ying Wa College

⦿ The former site of Hwa Nan College

⦿ The old scene of the Kuiqi campus of Fukien Christian University

The Western medical system was introduced during the spread of modern Christianity in Fujian, and many Western-style hospitals were opened. Based on treating illness, saving people, and spreading the gospel, medical classes and medical and nursing schools were set up to perform western medicine education, which nurtured a group of talents of western medicine for Fujian.

⦿ Foochow Medical Missionary Hospital

⦿ Hobe MacKay Hospital, the first western-style hospital in northern Taiwan founded by Canadian missionary George Leslie Mackay in Tamsui

The Christian Church has also founded many publishing houses (offices) in various places and created many newspapers and periodicals, which have promoted the development of Fujian's journalism and communication industry and its modernization. *Christian Advocate* was one of the earliest newspapers founded in Fujian and was greatly influenced by the newspaper industry at the time. The Chinese newspaper *Fu*, founded by Fuzhou native Huang Naishang, was the first Chinese western-style newspaper founded by Fujianese at the time.

⊙ The former site of the American Presbyterian Mission Press

主降生一千八百七十五年印

福建美以美新報

郇山使者

福州美華書局印

大清光緒元年二月初一日

目錄　文論　福州連環四季會議日期　福清縣連環單　興化連環會議單　福州連環第一季事畧　新設書坊　宣道機會　牛坑爲祈禱會事畧　女醫館啟　福音書院將落成　改正前報　敬抄上諭並兩宮皇太后懿旨　錄督轅牌示　遺詔　臺灣近事　電報無成　白鴿票大盛　遊東巖記　市雞說　壓塔斃命　美國天文士至福州　骰倒命數　負債潛逃　白首重婚　譯講禁鴉片大畧　希臘爲西國文學之祖　小孩穎悟　上帝遇人　聾啞幼孩　意外遭逢

第五卷

⦿ *Christian Advocate*, sample page

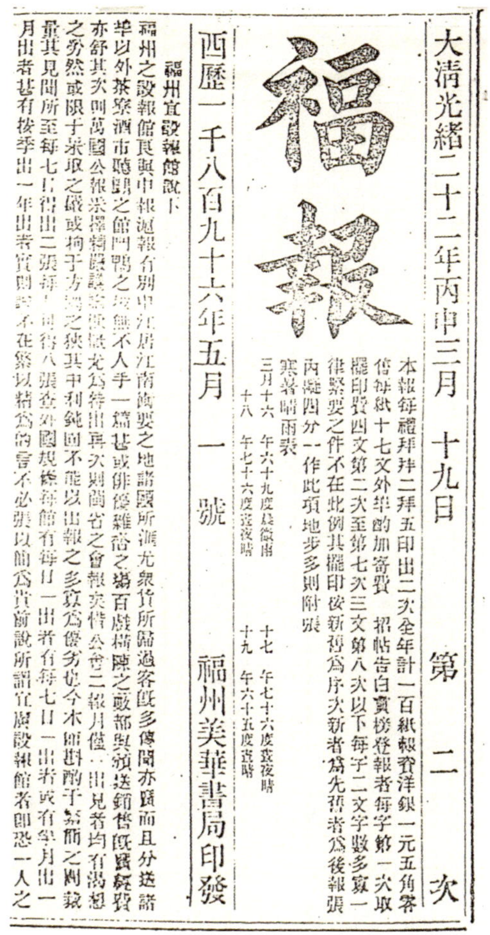

大清光緒二十二年丙申三月　十九日　第二次

福報

本報每禮拜二拜五印出二次全年計一百紙報資洋銀一元五角寄信每紙十七文外埠酌加寄費　招帖告白賣榜登報者每字第一次取擺印費四文第二次至第七次三文第八次以下每字二文字數多寡一律緊要之件不在此例其擺印按新舊爲序次新者爲先舊者爲後報張內擬四分一作此項地步多則附張

寒暑晴雨表

三月十六　午六十九度晨微雨　十七　午七十六度竟夜晴

十八　午七十六度竟夜晴　十九　午六十五度竟晴

西歷一千八百九十六年五月　一號　福州美華書局印發

福州宜設報館說下

福州之設報館良與申報滬報有別申江居江南衝要之地諸國所滙尤衆貨所歸過客既多傳聞亦廣而且分送諸埠以外茶寮酒市聽戲之館鬥鵪之場無不人手一篇甚或俳優雜沓之場百戲橫陳之處都與預送銷售既廣錢資亦舒其次則萬國公報崇揀精[illegible]尤爲特出再次則閩省之會報奐性公會二報月僅一出見者均有渴想之勢然或限于采取之儀或拘于方隅之狹其中利鈍固不能以出報之多寡爲優劣也今[illegible]最其見聞所至每七日得出二張每[illegible]得八張查外國規條報館有每日一出者有每七日一出者或有半月出一月出者甚有按季出一年出者實則[illegible]不在繁以精爲尚吾不必張以簡爲貴前說所謂宜廣設報館者即恐一人之

⦿ *Fu*, sample page

Charity was an essential part of the social services of modern Fujian Christianity. To realize the ideal of "God Bless China," many missionaries who came to Fujian and Taiwan paid attention to all social phenomena that might affect the mentality of the Chinese people. They tried to win people's hearts through secularized social improvement to achieve their missionary aims. Certain bad habits that contradict Western Christian culture naturally also fell into their scope of improvement and became the main content of their charity work.

Fuzhou Lingguang School for Blind Children, founded by British missionary Amy Oxlay in 1898, was the most influential school for blind children opened by Christian missionaries in Fujian. It adopted modern systematic educational modes and actively offered vocational training.

⦿ Exhortation to *Abandon Opium*, cover

⊙ Fuzhou Lingguang School for Blind Children

Tainan Blind School was the first school for the blind founded by the Presbyterian missionary William Campbell in Taiwan. It gave many blind children in Taiwan the opportunity to receive an education. It is a concrete manifestation of Christianity's participation in social charity and relief in Taiwan.

⊙ Portrait of William Campbell

The dairy cow test field founded by American missionary Edward Bliss in Shaowu

Dairy farming was a special part of the development of the Christian Church's affiliated public welfare undertakings and has profoundly impacted the future development of local animal husbandry, breeding, and dairy industries.

Westerners who came to China in modern times, especially the missionaries, conducted a comprehensive and in-depth investigation of cultural information in various regions and aspects of Fujian. Through more detailed field trips, they have extended their perspective to various objects that might reflect Chinese social culture. Their discussion and description of Chinese folk culture are undoubtedly important breakthroughs in the history of cultural exchanges between China and the West.

After arriving in Fuzhou in 1848, Robert Samuel Maclay, a missionary of the Methodist Episcopal Church, devoted himself to studying the Fuzhou dialect and compiled the *Alphabetic Dictionary of the Chinese Language in the Foochow Dialect* and *Manual of the Foochow Dialect*. He was one of the first missionaries who translated the New Testament into the Fuzhou dialect. Maclay built the Fuzhou Church of Heavenly Peace and was one of the pioneers of cultural exchanges between modern Fujian and the West. He also wrote *Life Among the Chinese*, which was an early observation and introduction to the social life of the Fujianese.

⦿ Portrait of Robert Samuel Maclay

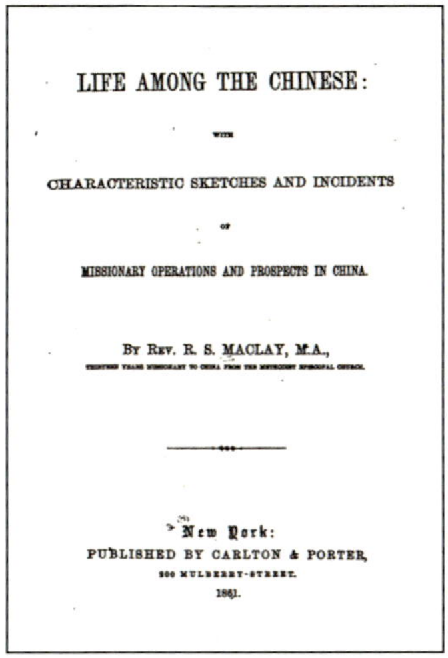

LIFE AMONG THE CHINESE:

WITH

CHARACTERISTIC SKETCHES AND INCIDENTS

OF

MISSIONARY OPERATIONS AND PROSPECTS IN CHINA.

BY REV. R. S. MACLAY, M.A.,

New York:

PUBLISHED BY CARLTON & PORTER,

1861.

⦿ *Life Among the Chinese*, cover

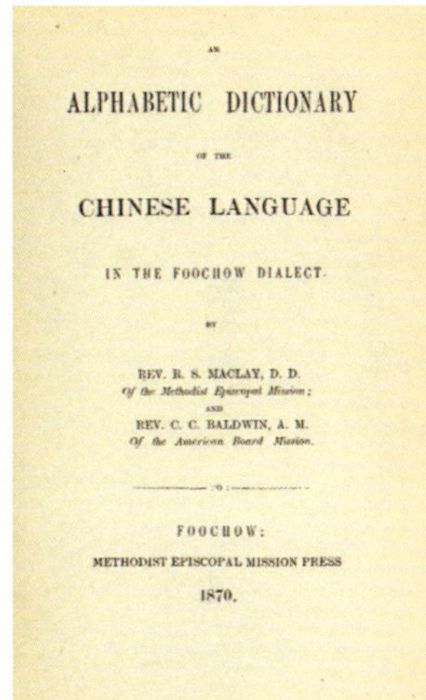

AN

ALPHABETIC DICTIONARY

OF THE

CHINESE LANGUAGE

IN THE FOOCHOW DIALECT.

BY

REV. R. S. MACLAY, D. D.

Of the Methodist Episcopal Mission;

AND

REV. C. C. BALDWIN, A. M.

Of the American Board Mission.

FOOCHOW:

METHODIST EPISCOPAL MISSION PRESS

1870.

⦿ *Fuzhou Dialect Romanization Dictionary*, cover

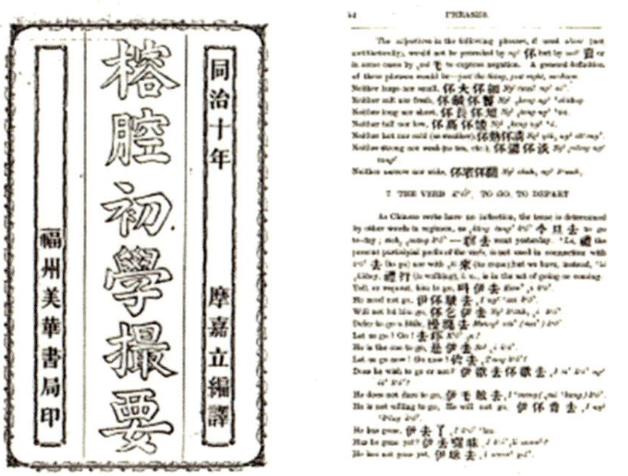

同治十年

榕腔初學撮要

摩嘉立編譯

福州美華書局印

Fifteen Initials.				Thirty-Three Finals.					
1	Liu	柳	L	1 Ch'ung	春	ung	17 Sieu (d)	燒	ieu
2	Piéng	邊	P	2 Hwa	花	wa	18 Ngüng	銀	üng
3	Kiu	求	K	3 Hiong	香	iong	19 Kong	釭	ong
4	K'e	氣	K'	4 Ch'iu (d)	秋	iu	20 Chi	之	i
5	Tá	低	T	5 Sang	山	ang	21 Tëng	東	ëng
6	P'ó	波	P'	6 K'ai	開	ai	22 Kau	郊	au
7	T'a	他	T'	7 Ka	嘉	a	23 Kwo (b)	過	wo
8	Cheng	曾	Ch	8 Ping	賓	ing	24 Sá	西	á
9	Nik	日	N	9 Hwang	歡	wang	25 Kio (c)	橋	io
10	Si	時	S	10 Kó	歌	ó	26 Kié	鷄	ié
11	Eng	鶯		11 Sü	須	ü	27 Siăng	聲	iăng
12	Mung	蒙	M	12 Pwí (a)	杯	wí	28 Ch'oi	催	oi
13	Ngü	語	Ng	13 Ku	孤	u	29 Ch'ë	初	ë
14	Ch'ok	出	Ch'	14 Teng	燈	eng	30 T'iéng	天	iéng
15	Hi	喜	H	15 Kwong	光	wong	31 K'iă	奇	iă
				16 Hwi	輝	wi	32 Wai	歪	wai
							33 Keu	溝	eu

⦿ *Manual of the Foochow Dialect*, cover and sample pages

The two representative works of American missionary Justus Doolittle that best describe the daily life and social customs of the Fujianese are *Fujianese–Social Life of the Chinese* and *A Vocabulary and Hand-book of the Chinese Language*, which deeply examine all aspects of the daily life of Fuzhou locals. They present the popular culture of the underclass in Fujian more delicately to Western readers.

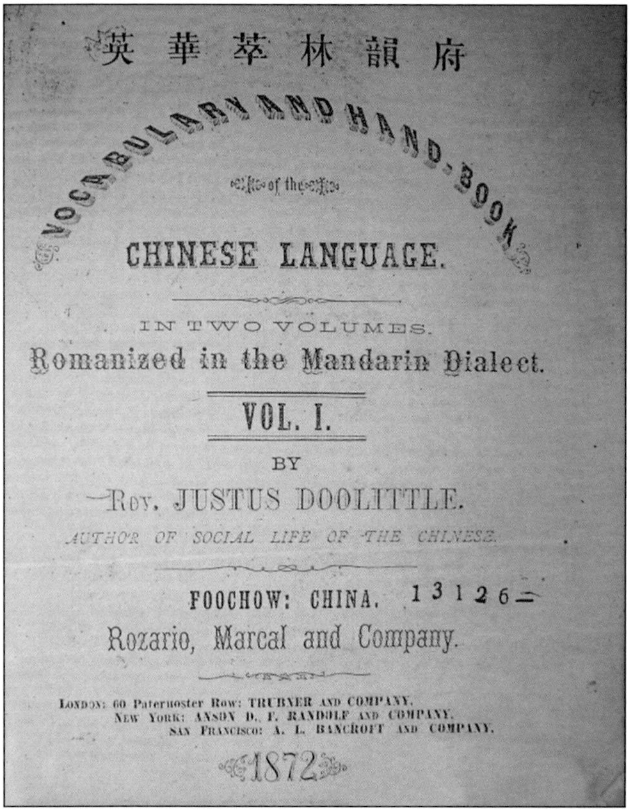

英華萃林韻府

VOCABULARY AND HAND-BOOK

of the

CHINESE LANGUAGE.

IN TWO VOLUMES.

Romanized in the Mandarin Dialect.

VOL. I.

BY

REV. JUSTUS DOOLITTLE.

AUTHOR OF SOCIAL LIFE OF THE CHINESE.

FOOCHOW: CHINA. 1 3 1 2 6 二

Rozario, Marcal and Company.

LONDON: 60 Paternoster Row: TRUBNER AND COMPANY.
NEW YORK: ANSON D. F. RANDOLF AND COMPANY.
SAN FRANCISCO: A. L. BANCROFT AND COMPANY.

1872

⦿ *A Vocabulary and Hand-book of the Chinese Language*, cover

John Thomson was a famous English traveler. He came to Fujian around 1870. He inspected the natural and cultural landscapes of Xiamen, Fuzhou, and northern Fujian along his journey. He recorded them in his album books, *Foochow and the Min River*, *Through China with a Camera*, and other works.

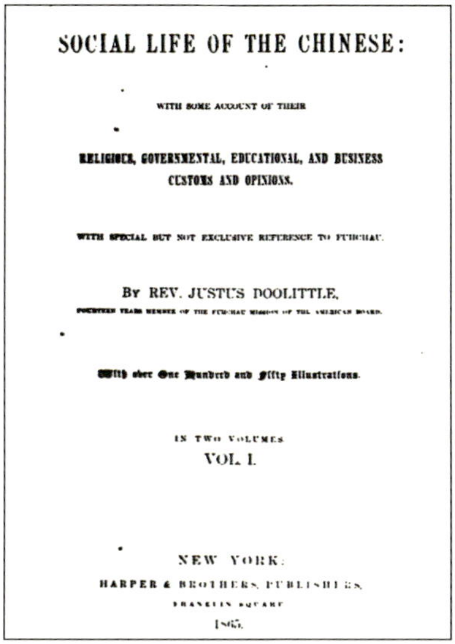

SOCIAL LIFE OF THE CHINESE:

WITH SOME ACCOUNT OF THEIR

RELIGIOUS, GOVERNMENTAL, EDUCATIONAL, AND BUSINESS CUSTOMS AND OPINIONS.

WITH SPECIAL BUT NOT EXCLUSIVE REFERENCE TO FUHCHAU.

BY REV. JUSTUS DOOLITTLE,

FOURTEEN YEARS MEMBER OF THE FUHCHAU MISSION OF THE AMERICAN BOARD.

With over One Hundred and Fifty Illustrations.

IN TWO VOLUMES.

VOL. I.

NEW YORK:

HARPER & BROTHERS, PUBLISHERS,

FRANKLIN SQUARE.

1865.

⊙ *Social Life of the Chinese*, cover

⊙ The Min River through the lens of John Thomson

Women and the Dan people (boat dwellers), the representatives of the underclass, were the focus of the missionaries' observation in Fujian. In their writings, there are often texts and pictures about Fujian women and the Dan people, which genuinely reproduce the life forms of the underclass of Fujian.

⊙ The Fujian Dan People in the eyes of modern Westerners

⦿ A group of pictures of Fujian women in the eyes of modern Westerners

Wanshou Bridge (now Fuzhou Jiefang Bridge) was the landmark of the economic prosperity area of the Min River Estuary. Foreign missionaries in China have paid more attention to Wanshou Bridge and its surrounding landscape. They recorded that there were various stalls on both sides of the bridge.

⊙ Pictures of Wanshou Bridge in the eyes of modern Westerners

In addition to traveling, living, and working in Fujian, Western missionaries also paid great heed to the economy of the local society and the daily production and life of the Fujianese. The fascinating historical pictures of local social and economic life in Fujian provide many historical details for people of today to examine the daily life of Fujianese in the late Qing Dynasty.

⦿ Agricultural production in the eyes of Westerners—irrigation via water wheel

⦿ Farmer processing rice with windmill

⦿ Cows squeezing cane sugar

⦿ Rice cultivation in rural Shaowu

⦿ Harvesting rice

⦿ Daily customs in the eyes of Westerners—Dragon boat racing

⊙ A bride and groom

⊙ Wedding ceremony

⊙ Going to a fair (market)

⦿ Prep for Chinese New Year

⦿ Rolling balls

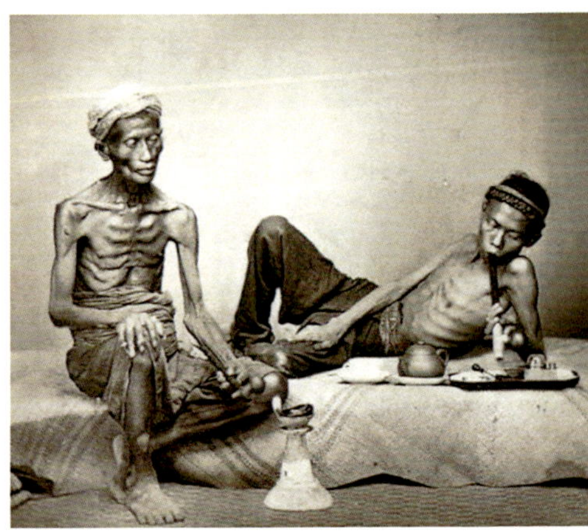

⦿ The vulgar custom of smoking opium

⊙ Worshipping ancestors

⊙ White rooster on a funeral coffin

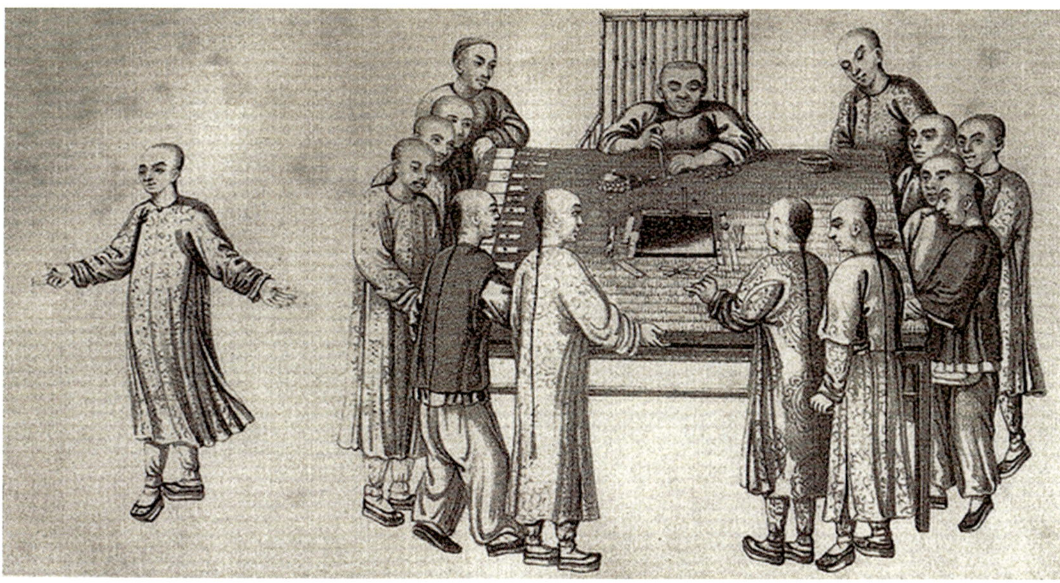

⊙ Gambling

⦿ A ladder of lights

⦿ The funeral team

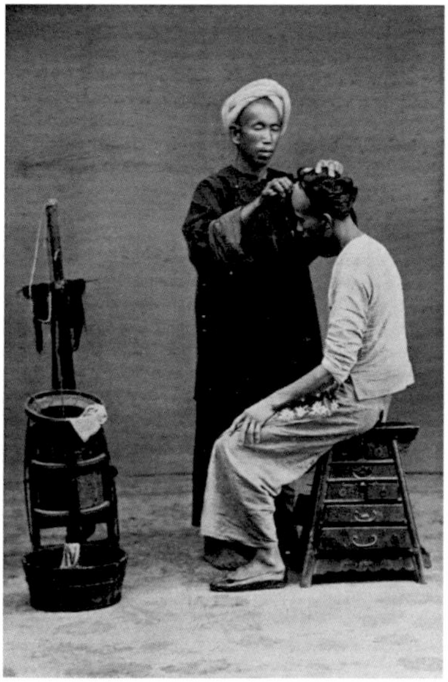

⊙ Market knowledge in the eyes of Westerners—Barber

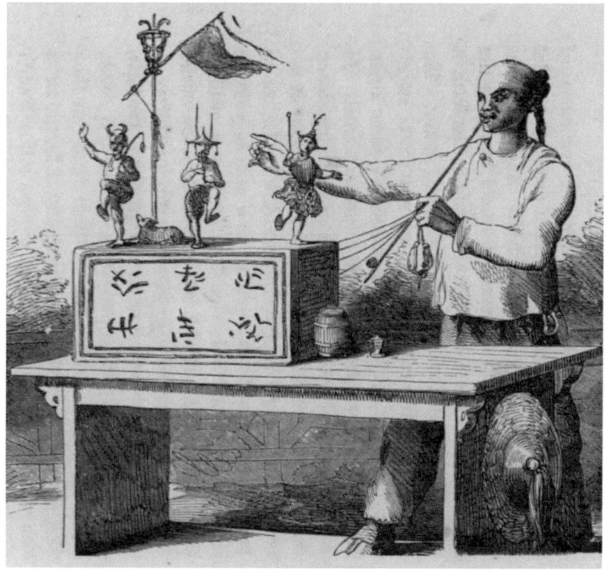

⊙ Artisan

⊙ A glimpse of a street in Fujian

⦿ Bearers

⦿ Street gambling

⦿ Street craftsman

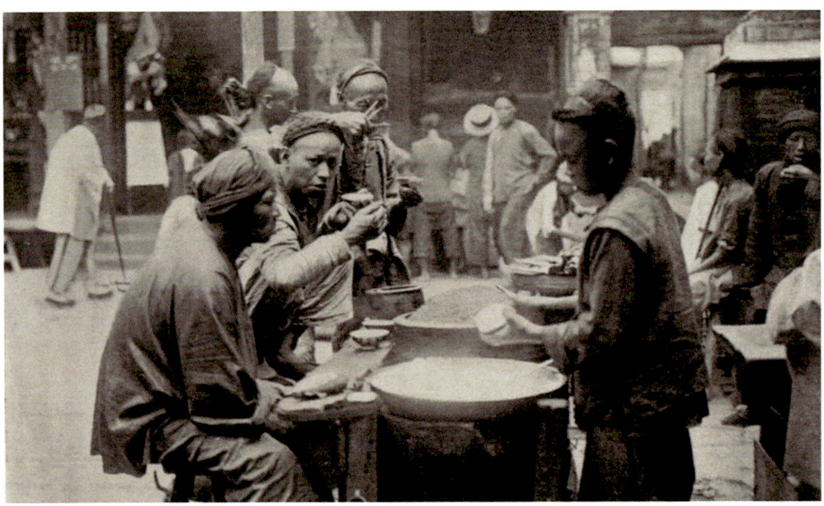

⦿ Street food stall

3 Pioneers of the Fujian—Fujian Shipbuilding Institution and Cultural Exchanges between China and the West

An important and notable sign of the import of modern western science, technology, and culture into Fujian is the establishment of the Fujian Shipping Bureau and the Foochow Shipbuilding Institution. Under the guidance of Western scientific and technological engineers, the shipyard introduced Western-style shipbuilding technology and independently built many warships and civilian ships, which strengthened the modern Fujian navy and maritime transport forces.

The Foochow Shipping Institution employed foreign teachers to give lectures and cultivate a legion of outstanding talents. It also sent four groups of international students to Western countries to further their studies and learn specialized knowledge. These Fujian students were the most direct communicators of Chinese and Western cultures in modern times and have played an outstanding role in the enlightenment of modern Chinese thought.

It was Zuo Zongtang who advocated the establishment of the Fujian Shipping Bureau. Under his vigorous advocacy, the imperial court accepted and implemented the proposal. The specific founder of Fujian Shipping Bureau was Shen Baozhen, who had dedicated himself to its establishment and operation and made outstanding contributions.

⦿ Portrait of Zuo Zongtang

⦿ Portrait of Shen Baozhen

In 1867, Foochow Shipbuilding Institution was founded. It was a new type of school with Western science and technology as its primary teaching content, and foreign teachers were directly hired to give lectures.

⦿ Foochow Shipbuilding Institution (Back Institution)

⦿ Fujian Shipping Bureau Panorama

Since the establishment of the Foochow Shipbuilding Institution, its courses were set entirely according to the Western curriculum, with different classes for different majors. All Chinese students studying there must master English and French to understand the content taught by foreign teachers, directly read various Western science and technology books, and learn and master modern Western advanced scientific and technological knowledge.

⦿ *Dragon Power*: China's first steel warship designed and manufactured by the Foochow Shipping Bureau

Many top students who graduated from the Foochow Shipbuilding Institution became teachers in emerging modern schools. In their teaching career, these modern Chinese intellectuals who first accepted Western science, technology, and culture, spread the Western science they had learned to various places and became the pioneers in introducing the advanced Western science and technology at the time.

As of the eve of the Revolution of 1911, the Foochow Shipbuilding Institution sent four batches of students to study in Europe, totaling 107 students. China's first batch of modern scientific and technological talents emerged among them. They eventually became the backbone of China's modern industrial and mining enterprises and naval construction in the late 19th and early 20th centuries, significantly developing China's modern science and technology.

The talents cultivated by the Foochow Shipbuilding Institution were an essential source of modern China's scientific, technological, diplomatic, and military skills. They played an important role in manufacturing modern warships, participating in anti-aggression naval battles, and building a coastal defense. They have also served in institutions functioning abroad and navies. Meanwhile, in the spread of Western science and the cultural exchange between China and the West, they were the bridge.

⦿ In 1877, the first batch of students of Foochow Shipbuilding Institution studying in Europe was admitted to the Royal Naval Academy, Greenwich, U.K.

4 The Westward Spread of Fujian Science—The Interaction among Fujian Translators, Western Sinologists, and Eastern and Western Science

In modern times, Fujian was leading the translation of Western literature and the introduction and dissemination of Western science in China. Yan Fu was one of the outstanding figures in those actions. Yan Fu, Lin Shu, and Gu Hongming were the famous Three Outstanding Fujianese in the history of modern cultural exchanges between China and the West. At the same time, Western sinology circles also researched and translated Chinese culture represented by Fujian science. Unlike the predecessors, this round of Fujian science spreading to the West has richer connotations and covers more diverse fields, which has extensively promoted the historical process of cultural exchanges between the East and the West.

Yan Fu (1854–1921), a native of Fuzhou, was a famous translator, educator, and thinker in modern times. During his teaching at Beiyang Naval Academy, he trained the first batch of naval talents in modern China, translated *Evolution and Ethics*, founded *Kuo Wen Pao*, systematically

⊙ Former residence of Yan Fu in Yangqi, Fuzhou

introduced Western democracy and science, publicized the idea of reform, and introduced Western sociology, political science, political economy, philosophy, and natural sciences to China. He was one of the "advanced Chinese" who sought truth from Western countries in modern China.

Though Yan's famous translation works are few in number, their great value and significance have influenced generations of Chinese. The purpose of his translations was to warn the world of the current disadvantages, so hundreds of millions of people would think. His selection of western books was meticulous. He linked traditional culture and ancient academic thought to the priorities of modern Chinese society and the needs of its current situation. He adopted the method of free translation to translate, shining the light of a thinker. He also frequently inserted enlightening and thought-provoking notes in his translation. His profound and intimate connection with modern Chinese ideology and culture is first-class, fully reflecting his desire to improve modern Chinese society. He held a rigorous translation attitude, too. Since *Evolution and Ethics*, he pioneered the translation standard of faithfulness, expressiveness, and elegance. Faithfulness means to stay faithful to the original work; expressiveness means smooth expressions; elegance means beautiful sentences. This remains the gold standard in the translation community.

⦿ Yan Fu's Tomb

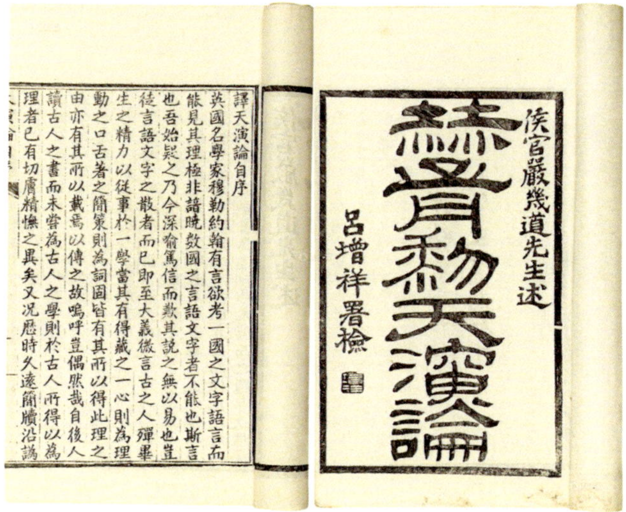

⦿ *Evolution and Ethics*, Chinese translation, cover and sample page

Driven by his strong patriotic zeal, Yan did not hesitate to raise the banner of spreading Western science to seek a way to save the country when the crisis of the Chinese nation was more serious than ever. His patriotism answered the call of the times. Through the sharp tool of translation, he widely spread Western science, the world outlook, and the methodology of the bourgeoisie. He inspired the Chinese to compare, think, and distinguish Chinese and Western societies and concepts, thus having a profound impact on the social progress at that time and in the future.

Lin Shu (1852–1924), a native of Fuzhou City, was a modern writer and translator. In his legendary translation career, he translated 246 Western novels, histories, academics, biographies, plays, stories, fables, and notes by noting other's oral interpretations, which caused a sensation in the Chinese literary arena. His translated western novels positively impacted the Chinese realm of thought and the literary arena. They have objectively opened the Chinese people with a window to understand western society, raised their anti-imperialist and anti-feudal consciousness, promoted their ideological awakening, had a positive impact on the transition of the modern Chinese realm of thought from old to new, corrected the public's views on the status of foreign literature, and elevated the social status of novels. His translations and introductions of Western literature have also directly cultivated the first generation of writers of modern Chinese literature.

⦿ Portrait of Lin Shu

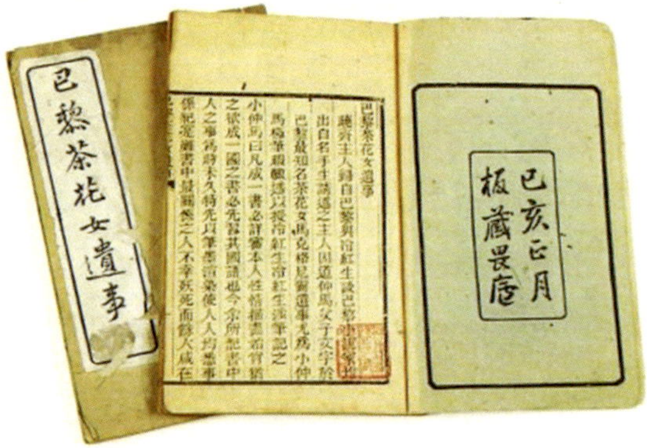

⦿ *La Dame Aux Camélias,* Chinese translation, sample page

Gu Hongming (1857–1928), whose ancestral home was Tongan, Fujian, was born in Penang Island in 1857. His mother was British. Gu was an erudite man who had learned both Chinese and Western cultures. He was a Chinese who received a complete British education and was proficient in English, French, German, Greek, Latin, and Sanskrit. Throughout his life, he took it as his mission to spread the quintessence of the Chinese culture to the West and promote China's morality and ethics. Westerners regard him as the representative of Chinese culture. He translated *The Analects of Confucius* and *The Doctrine of the Mean* into English, which were well received by western readers. In the history of cultural exchanges between China and

⦿ Portrait of Gu Hongming

the West, it was primarily Westerners who spread oriental culture. Gu is the most influential and authoritative among the Chinese who have directly disseminated oriental culture to the West.

As the first Chinese in modern China to spread Chinese culture to the West, Gu's ancestral home happened to be in Fujian, which is by no means accidental, but the inevitable result of Fujian's opening to the outside world since ancient times and the far-reaching impact of the cultural effect of many Fujianese emigrating to Southeast Asia in the Ming and Qing dynasties.

As the cultural exchanges between China and the West continued to deepen, excellent works of Fujian culture have also been translated and introduced to Western society in large numbers, setting off a trend of eastern science going west represented by the spread of Fujian culture in the West.

Chen Jitong (1851–1907), a native of Fuzhou, joined the Fuzhou Shipping Bureau in his early years and later studied law and politics in France. As he had worked and lived in Europe for a long time, Chen was proficient in French, English, German, and Latin, and had a deep understanding of Western culture. To enable Westerners to understand Chinese people and culture better, he authored and translated many French books, which were quite influential in the West then. His masterwork, *The Chinese as Painted*

⦿ Portrait of Chen Jitong

BIBLIOTHÈQUE CONTEMPORAINE

COLONEL TCHENG-KI-TONG

LES CHINOIS

PEINTS PAR EUX-MEMES

C·L

PARIS

CALMANN LÉVY, ÉDITEUR

1884

⦿ *The Chinese as Painted by Themselves*, French edition, sample page

by Themselves, gathers Chen's many speeches in Europe, showing Western readers an oriental civilization with a long culture and profound thinking. It caused a sensation in Europe. In addition, he also translated multiple tales in *Strange Tales from a Chinese Studio* into French and named it *Chinese Tales*, which was soon translated into English, Italian, German, and other languages after publication and gained popularity in Europe. Chen also created works such as *The Theater of China*, *Happiness of the Chinese*, and *The Yellow Man Novel*, which received positive responses in Western society.

Lin Yutang (1895–1976) was a famous writer, scholar, translator, and linguist in modern China. He was born in Banzai Town, Pinghe County, Zhangzhou City, Fujian Province. As a devout Christian, he was educated in church school since elementary school. He attended the church middle school in Xiamen and studied abroad in the U.S. and Germany. After returning to China, he taught at Tsinghua University, Peking University, and Xiamen University. He made tremendous literary achievements and is known as the "Master of Humor" in modern China. With his wit and humor, Lin actively promoted the spread of Chinese culture in the West. He was an important promoter of cultural exchanges between the East and the West in modern times.

⦿ Portrait of Lin Yutang

Former residence of Lin Yutang in Banzai Town, Pinghe

As Fuzhou and Xiamen were opened as trading ports, Fujian and the West became more closely connected in politics, economy, and culture. The excellent works written by Fujianese (including officials from other provinces serving in Fujian) began to be translated into languages of various countries and spread to the West. They have received a wide welcome in the West.

The Cheng-Zhu School is an excellent representative of Fujian's writings. In modern times, E. C. Bridgman, an American missionary from the Congregational Church, was the first to translate Zhu Xi's ideas into English. After coming to China in 1830, he studied Chinese with Robert Morrison. He founded the first English monthly magazine, *The Chinese Repository* in Guangzhou, which introduced China to Western readers, and he served as its editor-in-chief. When the Sino-U.S. Treaty of Wanghia (also known as the Treaty of Wangxia; Treaty of peace, amity, and commerce) was signed, he served as the translator for the U.S. In 1849, he first published the article *Notices of Chinese Cosmology* in the 18th issue of *The Chinese Repository*, translating some chapters about the universe, heaven and earth, sun and moon, and humans and animals in the *Book of Zhu Xi* into English, which marked the beginning of the West using direct source material as the basis to study Zhu Xi's ideas. Bridgman also translated the *Biography of Zhu Zi* by Gao Yu in the Qing Dynasty into English.

⦿ Portrait of E. C. Bridgman

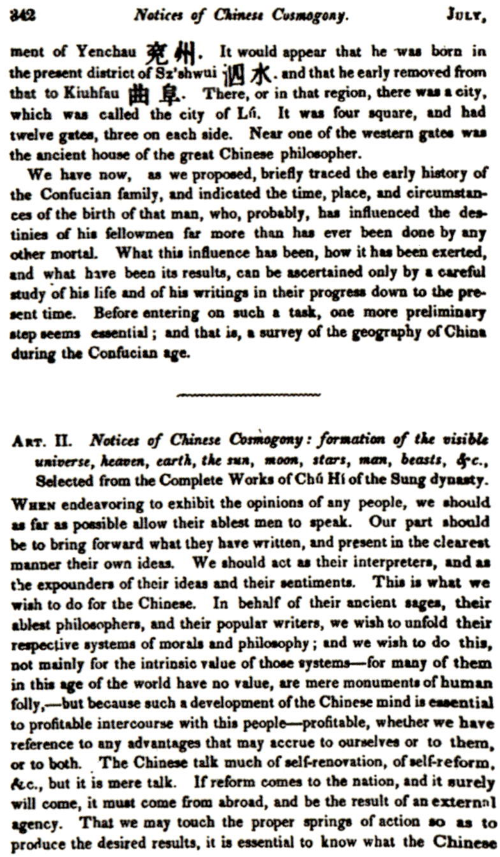

342 *Notices of Chinese Cosmogony.* JULY,

ment of Yenchau 兖州. It would appear that he was born in the present district of Sz'shwui 泗水, and that he early removed from that to Kiuhfau 曲阜. There, or in that region, there was a city, which was called the city of Lú. It was four square, and had twelve gates, three on each side. Near one of the western gates was the ancient house of the great Chinese philosopher.

We have now, as we proposed, briefly traced the early history of the Confucian family, and indicated the time, place, and circumstances of the birth of that man, who, probably, has influenced the destinies of his fellowmen far more than has ever been done by any other mortal. What this influence has been, how it has been exerted, and what have been its results, can be ascertained only by a careful study of his life and of his writings in their progress down to the present time. Before entering on such a task, one more preliminary step seems essential; and that is, a survey of the geography of China during the Confucian age.

ART. II. *Notices of Chinese Cosmogony: formation of the visible universe, heaven, earth, the sun, moon, stars, man, beasts, &c.,* Selected from the Complete Works of Chú Hí of the Sung dynasty.

WHEN endeavoring to exhibit the opinions of any people, we should as far as possible allow their ablest men to speak. Our part should be to bring forward what they have written, and present in the clearest manner their own ideas. We should act as their interpreters, and as the expounders of their ideas and their sentiments. This is what we wish to do for the Chinese. In behalf of their ancient sages, their ablest philosophers, and their popular writers, we wish to unfold their respective systems of morals and philosophy; and we wish to do this, not mainly for the intrinsic value of those systems—for many of them in this age of the world have no value, are mere monuments of human folly,—but because such a development of the Chinese mind is essential to profitable intercourse with this people—profitable, whether we have reference to any advantages that may accrue to ourselves or to them, or to both. The Chinese talk much of self-renovation, of self-reform, &c., but it is mere talk. If reform comes to the nation, and it surely will come, it must come from abroad, and be the result of an external agency. That we may touch the proper springs of action so as to produce the desired results, it is essential to know what the Chinese

⦿ *Notices of Chinese Cosmology*, sample page

William W. Rockhill (1854–1914), an American diplomat and sinologist, has conducted in-depth research on the transportation history of ancient China, Southeast Asia, and the West. In 1911, Rockhill and German sinologist Friedrich Hirth cooperated to translate *A Description of Barbarian Nations, Records of Foreign People* written by Zhao Rushi, a former manager of the Foreign Shipping Bureau in Fujian in the Song Dynasty, into English. In 1914, Rockhill translated part of the book *A Brief Account of Island Barbarians* written by Wang Dayuan, a navigator of the Yuan Dynasty, into English. Rockhill did much textual research on the place names in ancient Southeast Asia and the West in the above two books.

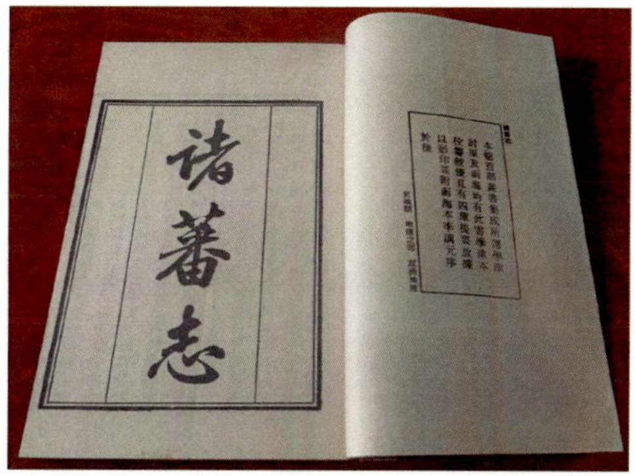

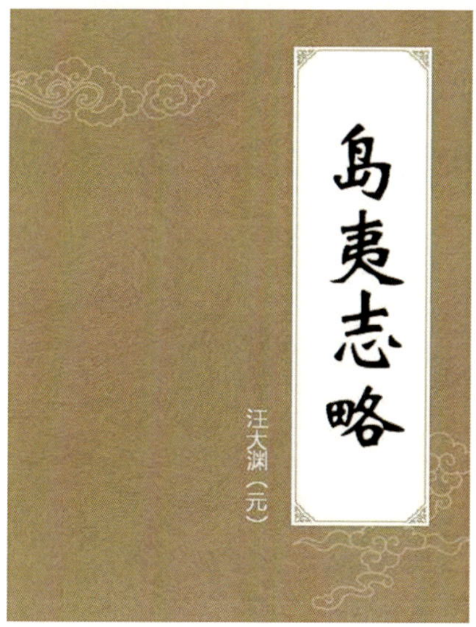

⦿ (ABOVE) Portrait of W. W. Rockhill

⦿ (ABOVE RIGHT) *A Description of Barbarian Nations, Records of Foreign People*, sample page

⦿ (RIGHT) *A Brief Account of Island Barbarians*, cover

Research on Eastern and Western Oceans is a history book on communications between China and the West written by Zhang Xie, a native of Longhai County, Zhangzhou, which followed the example of *A Description of Barbarian Nations, Records of Foreign People*. It was published in 1618 in 12 volumes. The book records the history, deeds, situations, resources, and transactions of overseas countries, mainly Southeast Asian countries, and the history of Western colonists plundering and enslaving the people of Southeast Asia. Therefore, it also attracted the attention of Western scholars. The Dutch sinologist W.P. Groeneveldt published his compilation *Notes on the Malay Archipelago and Malacca* in 1877, which translated and introduced part of *Research on Eastern and Western Oceans*. In 1893, the famous French Sinology magazine *Melanges* published an article introducing *Notes on the Malay Archipelago and Malacca.*

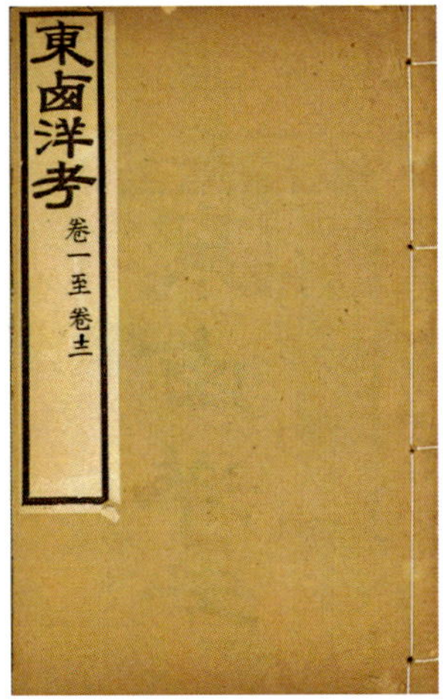

⦿ *Research on Eastern and Western Oceans*, cover

⦿ Portrait of W.P. Groeneveldt

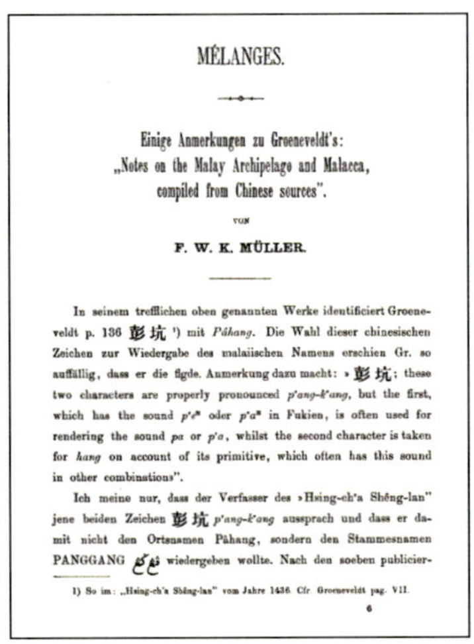

MÉLANGES.

Einige Anmerkungen zu Groeneveldt's:
„Notes on the Malay Archipelago and Malacca,
compiled from Chinese sources".

von

F. W. K. MÜLLER.

In seinem trefflichen oben genannten Werke identificiert Groeneveldt p. 136 彭坑 [1]) mit *Pâhang*. Die Wahl dieser chinesischen Zeichen zur Wiedergabe des malaiischen Namens erschien Gr. so auffällig, dass er die flgde. Anmerkung dazu macht: »彭坑: these two characters are properly pronounced *p'ang-k'ang*, but the first, which has the sound *p'ê*ⁿ oder *p'a*ⁿ in Fukien, is often used for rendering the sound *pa* or *p'a*, whilst the second character is taken for *hang* on account of its primitive, which often has this sound in other combinations".

Ich meine nur, dass der Verfasser des »Hsing-ch'a Shêng-lan" jene beiden Zeichen 彭坑 *p'ang-k'ang* aussprach und dass er damit nicht den Ortsnamen Pâhang, sondern den Stammesnamen PANGGANG ڤڠڬڠ wiedergeben wollte. Nach den soeben publicier-

1) So im: „Hsing-ch'a Shêng-lan" vom Jahre 1436. Cfr. Groeneveldt pag. VII.

6

⦿ *An Introduction to Notes on the Malay Archipelago and Malacca* in the *Melanges* in 1893

Washing Away of Wrongs, also known as *Collected Cases of Injustice Rectified*, was written by Song Ci (1186–1249), a Fujian native in the Song Dynasty. As the world's first systematic work on forensic medicine, it is hailed as a "great cultural milestone" by Western medical historians. In 1874, Herbert Allen Giles (1845–1935), a famous British sinologist, translated and published it in 1874, and it was serialized in three parts in *The China Review*. In 1924, Giles's translation of *Washing Away of Wrongs* was published in a separate edition and regarded as the most influential and authoritative English translation.

⦿ Portrait of Herbert Allen Giles

⦿ *Washing Away of Wrongs*, cover

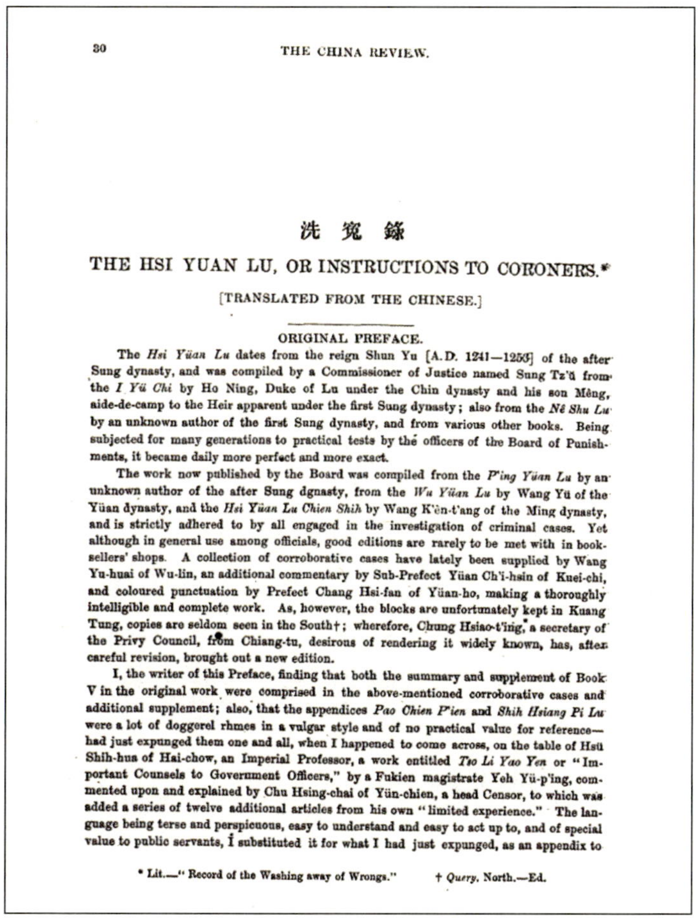

30 THE CHINA REVIEW.

洗 冤 錄

THE HSI YUAN LU, OR INSTRUCTIONS TO CORONERS.*

[TRANSLATED FROM THE CHINESE.]

ORIGINAL PREFACE.

The *Hsi Yüan Lu* dates from the reign Shun Yu [A.D. 1241—1253] of the after Sung dynasty, and was compiled by a Commissioner of Justice named Sung Tz'ŭ from the *I Yü Chi* by Ho Ning, Duke of Lu under the Chin dynasty and his son Mêng, aide-de-camp to the Heir apparent under the first Sung dynasty; also from the *Nê Shu Lu* by an unknown author of the first Sung dynasty, and from various other books. Being subjected for many generations to practical tests by the officers of the Board of Punishments, it became daily more perfect and more exact.

The work now published by the Board was compiled from the *P'ing Yüan Lu* by an unknown author of the after Sung dgnasty, from the *Wu Yüan Lu* by Wang Yü of the Yüan dynasty, and the *Hsi Yüan Lu Chien Shih* by Wang K'ên-t'ang of the Ming dynasty, and is strictly adhered to by all engaged in the investigation of criminal cases. Yet although in general use among officials, good editions are rarely to be met with in booksellers' shops. A collection of corroborative cases have lately been supplied by Wang Yu-huai of Wu-lin, an additional commentary by Sub-Prefect Yüan Ch'i-hsin of Kuei-chi, and coloured punctuation by Prefect Chang Hsi-fan of Yüan-ho, making a thoroughly intelligible and complete work. As, however, the blocks are unfortunately kept in Kuang Tung, copies are seldom seen in the South†; wherefore, Chung Hsiao-t'ing, a secretary of the Privy Council, from Chiang-tu, desirous of rendering it widely known, has, after careful revision, brought out a new edition.

I, the writer of this Preface, finding that both the summary and supplement of Book V in the original work were comprised in the above-mentioned corroborative cases and additional supplement; also, that the appendices *Pao Chien P'ien* and *Shih Hsiang Pi Lu* were a lot of doggerel rhmes in a vulgar style and of no practical value for reference—had just expunged them one and all, when I happened to come across, on the table of Hsü Shih-hua of Hai-chow, an Imperial Professor, a work entitled *Tso Li Yao Yen* or "Important Counsels to Government Officers," by a Fukien magistrate Yeh Yü-p'ing, commented upon and explained by Chu Hsing-chai of Yün-chien, a head Censor, to which was added a series of twelve additional articles from his own "limited experience." The language being terse and perspicuous, easy to understand and easy to act up to, and of special value to public servants, I substituted it for what I had just expunged, as an appendix to

* Lit.—"Record of the Washing away of Wrongs." † *Query*, North.—Ed.

⦿ Giles's translation of *Washing Away of Wrongs* published in *The China Review*

Feng Menglong (1574–1646) of the Ming Dynasty was the magistrate of Shouning, Fujian. He authored *The Story of the Three Unselfish Literati*, a classic of ancient Chinese novels. Westerners showed great interest in it and have tried translating it. Stanislas Aignan Julien, (1797–1873), born in Orleans, France, in 1797, studied and taught at the Institute of France. He devoted himself to research and was proficient in Chinese. He translated such Chinese classics as *Mencius*, *The Three Character Classic*, *The Orphan of Zhao*, *The Story of the Western Chamber*, *The Two Fair Cousins*, and *The Exploitation of the Works of Nature*. He was the first French sinologist to translate Feng Menglong's novel *The Story of the Three Unselfish Literati*.

Gustave Schlegel (1840–1903) was a famous Dutch sinologist, born in the Netherlands in 1840 and later became the first professor of Chinese and Chinese literature at Leiden University. In 1885, he came to China as a translator for the Dutch government and worked in Xiamen and other places. He translated *The Oil-Peddler Wins the Queen of Flowers* in Feng Menglong's *Stories to Awaken the World*.

In addition, British consul R.W. Hurst also introduced *The Story of the Three Unselfish Literati* to Western readers during his work and travel in Fujian, which was published in *The China Review* in 1886 and 1887.

⦿ Portrait of Stanislas Aignan Julien

⦿ Portrait of Gustave Schlegel

78 THE CHINA REVIEW.

it is very likely that his doctrines would have been broader and not so dry as those of Confucius. Considered as a man, his character was nobler and more dauntless than that of Ch'ung-ni. He never made an official lie. Regarded as an active statesman he was far superior to the sage. The latter was in office only four years and did not attain to the position of chief-minister in Lu, whilst Tsze-ch'an was 23 years (not 26, as the Sze ki has it) minister in Chăng, and held out under the most difficult circumstances, toiling and labouring practically for the welfare of his country, whilst Confucius was dreaming of an ideal government which never could be realised. He might well have said to his young friend,

'Grau Freund ist deine Theorie,
Grün ist des Lebens goldner Baum.'

There have been great men in China besides Confucius, and Tsze-ch'an is one of them. 'He was a virtuous man who loved his people and served his ruler faithfully.' Sze ki, chap. 42.

E. R. Eichler.

STORY OF THE THREE UNSELFISH LITERATI.

[The following is a literal translation of the first story contained in the Chin Ku Chi Kuan (今古奇觀) or Curious Stories of the Present and the Past. This book is a collection of tales which by their brevity and simplicity contrast favourably with the prolixity and inordinate length for which Chinese novels in general are so remarkable].

The downfall of the branches of a Judas tree restored the fortunes of a family.
In the Hua wo pavilion brothers slept on the same couch.
In times past, elder brothers lived with younger.
For thousands of years unbrotherly persons feel shame when they recite the poem about the beanstalks.

The object of the above lines is to commend brotherly love, and therein are contained three trite allusions, which I will now explain one by one. To begin with the first, the downfall of the branches of a Judas tree restored the fortunes of a family.

Once upon a time there were three brothers named Tien, who had lived and messed together from their childhood. The eldest married a wife who was known as Mrs. Tien Ta; the second also married, and his wife went by the name of Mrs. Tien Erh. The two sisters-in-law were on affectionate terms and never had a word of difference. Now the third brother was but a child, and lived with his brothers and sisters-in-law, but when he grew to manhood, he also married, and his wife was known as Mrs. Tien San. Now this lady was not a paragon of virtue; and besides, she gave herself airs by reason of being possessed of a considerable dowry. When she saw her husband's relations cooking and eating in common, and keeping no check of each one's private expenditure, she objected to this system, being fond of better fare. So she gave her husband no peace day or night, saying, 'Your common exchequer and property are all managed by your brothers; the receipts and disbursements are all unknown to you; they know what they are about, you are kept in the dark. If they use one article, and charge for ten, or use ten and charge for a hundred, how much wiser are you? Though for the present you may live together, still in the long run you must separate. Supposing

⦿ Hurst's article in *The China Review* introducing *The Story of the Three Unselfish Literati*

Summary

The Maritime Silk Road is an important link between the East and the West. The communication and interaction between the East and the West commenced in the Song and Yuan Dynasties. They entered a new round of progress in the Age of Discovery under the background of the colonial expansion of Western colonialist countries. The outbreak of the Chinese rites controversy in the late Ming and early Qing dynasties directly halted the cultural exchanges between the East and the West. Over 100 years later, when they both opened the door to exchanges again, the world pattern had undergone drastic changes. There is no more equal exchange and equal dialogue between China and the West through the Maritime Silk Road.

Centuries of exchanges and interactions between Fujian and the West via the Maritime Silk Road have given us many positive and beneficial inspirations. These historical experiences are a valuable reference for today's reconstruction of the 21st Century Maritime Silk Road.

Primarily, the reconstruction of the 21st Century Maritime Silk Road is based on the first economic, spiritual, and cultural exchanges. In other words, the 21st Century Maritime Silk Road not only carries the function of goods circulation but also undertakes the mission of cultural exchange.

Then, it must be a path of two-way interaction with peaceful development and equality. History has taught us that the construction of the 21st Century Maritime Silk Road should inherit the Maritime Silk Road spirit of harmonious exchanges, mutual benefits, equal dialogues, coexistence, and shared prosperity, to respond to the increasingly obvious trend of globalization actively.

Next, we should strengthen our own cultural construction and enhance China's cultural soft power. To rebuild the 21st Century Maritime Silk Road, we must have cultural soft power that attracts foreigners to learn Chinese culture. Only when the Chinese culture is well established, and the image of cultural power is reshaped can China better attract the world to understand and learn Chinese culture.

Finally, the reconstruction of the 21st Century Maritime Silk Road needs to focus on the cultural connections between various regions in China. Today, regarding how each place can be integrated into the construction of the Maritime Silk Road, we should look at the problem from a connected and dynamic perspective and focus on exploring the cultural connections and the context of the times between cities and regions. In this way, we can present the connotation and characteristics of this new Maritime Silk Road in a connected way, look at every detail and element in the construction of the new Maritime Silk Road with a holistic and developmental perspective, and better serve the national strategic decision-making and the establishment of China's international image.

References

[Holland] Blusse, Leonard. *History of Sino-Dutch Communication*. Translated by Zhuang Guotu and Cheng Shaogang. Holland Crossroads Publishing House, 1989.

[Holland] Bontekoe, Willem. *Memorable Description of the East Indian Voyage*. Translated by Yao Nan. Zhonghua Book Company, 1982.

Chen, Kaijun et al., trans. *The Travels of Marco Polo*. Fujian Science and Technology Press, 1981.

Fang, Hao. *The History of Communications between China and the West.* Yuelu Publishing House, 1987.

Fujian Local History Research Office, Department of History, Fujian Normal University. *Selected Historical Materials of the Opium War in Fujian and Taiwan*. Fujian People's Publishing House, 1982.

Fujian Museum. *The Long Silk Road: Relics of the Maritime Silk Road*. Fujian Education Press, 2013.

Halde, Jean-Baptiste Du, ed. *The Collection of Chinese Books of the Jesuits—Chinese Memoirs* (*Volumes 1–6*). Translated by Geng Sheng et al. Elephant Press, 2001–2005.

He, Gaoji, trans. *The Travels of Friar Odoric*, Zhonghua Book Company, 1981.

[British] Hudson, G. F. *Europe and China*. Translated by Li Shen et al. Zhonghua Book Company, 2nd ed., 2004.

Jiang, Shusheng, trans. *The Zeelandia Diaries* (*Volumes 1–3*). Tainan City Government, 1999–2003.

Li, Tiangang, trans. *Impression of the Imperial Cities of the Qing Dynasty—British Copper Prints in the 19th Century*. Shanghai Ancient Books Publishing House, 2002.

Liao, Dake. *Fujian Overseas Traffic History*. Fujian People's Publishing House, 2002.

Lin, Jinshui, and Xie Bizhen. *History of Fujian's Foreign Cultural Exchanges*. Fujian Education Press, 1997.

Lin, Jinshui. "A Preliminary Study of Min Zhong Zhu Gong Zeng Shi." *Religious Culture* 3, Oriental Publishing House, 1998.

Lin, Jinshui. "The Dissemination and Influence of Cheng-zhu School in the West during the Ming and Qing Dynasties." *Cheng-zhu School Journal* 6, 7. Huangshan Publishing House, 1994, 1995.

Lin, Jinshui. *The List of Friendships between Aleni and Fujian Literati and Officialdom, Sino-Foreign Relations History Series*. Vol. 5. Bibliography Literature Publishing House, 1996.

Lin, Renchuan. *Private Maritime Trade in the Late Ming and Early Qing Dynasties*. East China Normal University Press, 1987.

Liu, Yijie. "Research on the Origin of Fujian Ships." *Research on the History of Maritime Communication*, no. 2 (2016).

Maritime Silk Road Research Center. *Crossing the Ocean—China's Maritime Silk Road Eight Cities Cultural Heritage Exhibition*. Ningbo Publishing House, 2012.

State Administration of Cultural Heritage. *Maritime Silk Road*. Cultural Relics Press, 2014.

[Spanish] Mendoza, Juan Gonzalez De. *History of the Great Chinese Empire*. Translated by He Gaoji. Zhonghua Book Company, 1998.

[American] McFoy. "Study of People Traveling to Western Fujian Before the Eighteenth Century." Translated by Jin Yunming. *Fujian Culture* 2, no. 2.

[Portuguese] Pinto, Fernão Mendes et al. *Portuguese in China*. Translated by Wang Suoying. Macao Cultural Affairs Bureau, etc., 1998.

[American] Ross, Sarah. *Tea Thief: The Chinese Tea that Changed World History*. Translated by Meng Chi. Social Sciences Literature Publishing House, 2010.

Wang, Yaohua, and Xie Bizhen. *Fujian-Taiwan Maritime Traffic Research*. China Social Sciences Press, 2000.

Wu, Weiwei, and Lin Jinshui. "Fujian and Cultural Exchanges between China and the West in the Ming and Qing Dynasties: The Historical Opportunity and Contemporary Enlightenment of the Maritime Silk Road." *Research on the History of Maritime Relations*, no. 2 (2015).

Wu, Wenliang, and Wu Youxiong. *Quanzhou Religious Stone Carvings (revised and enlarged edition)*. Science Press, 2005.

Wu, Xiangxiang. *Catholic Literature (1–3 Editions)*. Taiwan Student Book Company, 1964–1972.

Xu, Minglong. *Huang Jialue, and Early French Sinology*. Zhonghua Book Company, 2004.

Xu, Xiaowang. *General History of Fujian (Volumes 1–5)*. Fujian People's Publishing House, 2006.

Zhang, Xinglong. *Compilation of Historical Materials of Communications between China and the West (Volumes 1–6)*. Zhonghua Book Company, 1977–1979.

Zhu, Qianzhi. *The Influence of Chinese Philosophy on Europe*. Fujian People's Publishing House, 1983.

About the Chief Editor

Mr. Xie Bizhen, Professor and Doctoral Supervisor of Fujian Normal University, Director of the Fujian-Taiwan Regional Research Center of Fujian Normal University, a key research base of humanities and social sciences of the Ministry of Education. His main research focuses on Chinese overseas transportation and trade history, the history of Sino-Japanese relations, and the local history of Fujian.

About the Author

Wu Weiwei is a historian with a Ph.D. from Shunchang, Fujian. He is a research fellow and doctoral supervisor at the Fujian-Taiwan Regional Research Center and the Collaborative Innovation Center for Cross-Strait Cultural Development at Fujian Normal University. Wu's research focuses on the history of maritime transportation, the local history of Fujian and Taiwan, and the history of Christianity in China. He has published ten books and over 50 academic papers and has directed and participated in numerous research projects. Wu has received many awards and honors for his research and is recognized as an outstanding young researcher at Fujian Normal University.